SCOTLAND'S
UNTOLD
STORIES

Also by Leonard Low:

Largo's Untold Stories
St Andrews' Untold Stories

The Weem Witch
The Battle of St Monans

SCOTLAND'S UNTOLD STORIES

LEONARD LOW

GUARDBRIDGE BOOKS
ST ANDREWS, SCOTLAND

Published by Guardbridge Books,
St Andrews, Fife, United Kingdom.

http://guardbridgebooks.co.uk

Scotland's Untold Stories

Cover Photograph: Urquhart Castle on Loch Ness, © Lian Deng | Dreamstime.com

ISBN: 978-1-911486-60-2

Foreword

I am a storyteller. There, I've said it! A throwback from the digital age to the old fireside historian, I'm someone who takes great pride in my country's achievements. But I also have a fanatical interest in its heroic disasters, of which in Scotland there were many! My interests and lectures come from the prime sources, sometimes books hundreds of years old. I want to tell the original story: stories have been forgotten or rewritten by author upon author until the original tale is but a shadow of what it was on the original charter. My interests stem from a much darker element than the tourist fodder about Scotland you are used to.

I like to chase stories back to where they originated, the first-edition volumes from whence they began their life on paper and in files.

To be blunt to my reader, I thrive in the pages of the ugly side of history, dark mysteries and historical terrors that stick in the mind long after hearing. With my previous books, I have been tagged in the press with many dubious titles, but one article in the *Dundee Courier* exclaimed "Leonard Low brings dead history alive" and I do like that! It explains in a wee sentence what I'm trying to achieve, to preserve these stories for future generations. These tales you're about to read in this volume are all true, and thought-provoking.

Some tales are utterly tragic, some involve the innocent at the right time but just the wrong place! Some characters are complete villains in the pages of history but were more famous being dead than alive. With others their echo from the past still carries on today, in legend turned to modern folklore with the roots of the true story very hard to find! Lost in the turmoil of time.

I have dug deep in the historical accounts in my own library of 17th-century books about Scotland to bring you long-forgotten stories that have lain hidden in my opinion for far too long. As with my previous works I try to be thorough in my research and try to piece together a story like a jigsaw. I sometimes where permitted add my own thoughts to help paint a better picture for the reader, but again these locations are still there for you to discover like I did: there is indeed a darker side of this magnificent country called Scotland. But this book is for you, the reader! For you to read the chapters you now hold, then find and visit, and stand in awe (or horror) regarding the events of what happened in these places...like I did...in the places of Scotland where the chapters happened. Do enjoy!

—Leonard Low

Acknowledgements

My thanks again to the many foot soldiers in my camp who support me in one way or another, please accept my gratitude for staying with me on this erratic journey through the darkest side of history in my printed works so far!...

Many thanks to these specimens from the Dark Dungeons of Dr Frankenstein's laboratories...Bruce Marshall, Ian Muirhead, William Mclean, Steven (Sherpa boy) Gilfeather, John Van Dieken, Jamie Rowbotham, Irish (Jocky) Richard, Dave Baxter and Billy Morris, Anya and Hugh Mackay, Dave Low and Linda Whiteford, Rog and Pamela and Trent Marshall. My special Goblins...Callum and Kirsty Low and Amber...All at *Haunted Magazine* where *The Lowdown of Witches/Hauntings* has its residency and not forgetting continual coverage in mainstream papers and magazines...*East Fife Mail*, *Courier*, *Scotsman*, *Daily Record*, *The Sun*, *St Andrews in Focus* magazine, *Evening Standard* and *Fortean Times* magazine...My love to Ruth for putting up with a library of ugly 500-year-old books, with my herd of Scottish Dumpy hens and with my new midlife crisis of collecting full sets of medieval armour! And of course,...with me!

Thanks to BBC York Radio, BBC Scotland, BBC Alba and the Outlander team for Men in Kilts programme with Sam Heughan and Graham McTavish...great laughs were had! Secrets were kept! (your sheekrets are shafe Sham) HA!

Nobody ever gives them credit. But a small newsagent in Largo approached me to sell my books. Andy Bones shop sits in Largo Bay nestled between two fantastic pubs: The Crusoe and the Railway Tavern. The turnover in books sold from here and being my hometown has been amazing with the dark days in publishing now on us, I need all the help I can get…A massive thanks from me!

This, my latest book, was due again with Steve Savage Publications LTD around June 2020. But Corona Virus arrived in Scotland in March via a Rugby international in Italy. Scots supporters back home became ill, the dying started.

Life as we knew it changed. The publishing companies were hit hard…Steve Savage himself took ill and after he emerged from hospital his business and this book were secondary to his own recovery. With my new publisher I hope to eclipse what I did with Steve. 15 years ago I walked into his office, I got my ten minutes to tell The Weem Witch…he took a chance, published it, and the book sold in the thousands and took me on this journey…Four books later…I thank you Steve. Recover well my friend…one day we will hold whiskeys again…

—Leonard Low, August 7th in Leven 3.30 am 2020…Keeping a hungry head-butting ginger cat from running over my computer keys as in the background outside the crows of my giant Cockerel "Eric Chinbags" greets the sunrise…

CONTENTS

Chapter 1

Give A Big Hand For Alan Clephane

In 1888 Glasgow, a major exhibition took place in the Bishop's Castle of Glasgow. The castle was actually a reproduction of a 12th or 13th century building. It was specially built in Kelvingrove Park, built for one purpose and designed by Mr James Sellars as part of the "Glasgow International Exhibition of 1888". It was to hold a display of Scotland's greatest treasures and memorials, for the first time all gathered together in one place for display.

The sword of Robert the Bruce, the Wallace sword, Roman artefacts and many letters from Mary Queen of Scots and Jacobean treasures filled the exhibit. Interesting fossils, Pictish stone carvings and Robert Burns' letters made impressive and colourful displays. But one of the display items, a strange, very weathered and unsightly looking mechanical arm, sat mainly unobserved because of its ugly rusting posture.

Looks can deceive, and this item certainly does. It has an amazing history and deserves its own position and chapter in this volume of *Scotland's Untold Stories*.

It reminds us of a very popular TV series and the bestselling books of the author George R. R. Martin: The Game of Thrones phenomenon!

In 1314 the fight for Scottish independence was leading to the Battle of Bannockburn. Edward Bruce had made an agreement with the English occupiers of Stirling Castle, that if they were not relieved by June 1314 by the English army, they would surrender the castle to the Scots. This deal helped to provoke Edward II of England into moving north. Robert Bruce was furious at his brother's action; they had avoided a full confrontation with the English over eight years, perfecting guerrilla warfare to level the forces and castles occupied by the English.

Robert Bruce knew he had nothing like what the English could bring in the way of armed horse and archers on to a battlefield. But the deal was set, and Bruce had to train his men and prepare for the coming confrontation.

Clan chiefs and Lairds emptied castles and glens to answer their king's call to arms. From Fife came the laird of Lundy Castle in Largo and the Earl of Rothes in North Fife with the Lyndsey Clan. In all, over 3,000 men were raised from Fife. One such laird to join this army was Alan Clephane from Cupar. He owned a small estate and castle called Carslogie.

King Robert Bruce would split his army under four leaders, himself in reserve, his brother Edward Bruce and the Black Douglas at the front, and his nephew Randolph. The Fife men joined the Douglas battalion with pike and axes; each battalion was over 5,000 men and when the action started, they were in the thick of the fighting.

The men had been trained to compact themselves into a human hedgehog of spears with the leader of each battalion in the middle seated on a horse. With rigorous training over the months before the English arrived, they had created a mobile force that could advance quickly in an impenetrable wall of spears spiked with iron tips. They called these mobile divisions "schiltrons".

The English arrived, and a two-day battle began. Edward II had picked the wrong land to camp on for his thousands of knights and archers. The land was a marsh and tidal inlets flooded the area, making it completely unsuitable for cavalry. The Scots attacked on foot with their schiltrons of three-metre-long spears and plucked the knights from their horses; it was a slaughter. Men trapped by fallen horses and stuck in mud unable to reach the enemy, the knights blocking the view for archers who were in the wrong position to shoot upon the Scots – they would hit their own men! The English dead piled up high as they could not manoeuvre from their tight position on this unsuitable ground. They lost thousands of their bravest knights, and their army disintegrated fleeing the field.

The day was won against the English, who had an army four times the size of Bruce's forces. Tactics and training had won the day.

Many English knights had been captured and ransoms were issued to stately homes, where lucrative sums of money were exchanged for the shamed knights' safe return. But Bruce's forces had also lost many men in that killing field at Bannockburn, especially when it was hotly contested in the second day's final confrontation. Many had received grievous wounds.

One such casualty was Alan Clephane from Cupar: he

had emptied the garrison of Carslogie Castle and fought in the Black Douglas battalion in the thick of the action. He had marshalled his own men around him and at an early part of the engagement had lost his right hand, his sword hand being cut off at the wrist by an English knight's war axe. Seeing their laird wounded, his men rallied to his protection. The stump was wrapped up in linen and Alan Clephane, although grievously wounded, continued the struggle using his left hand with a pike.

The battle was won, and the debris of war now settled as wounds were treated and the dead were honoured and buried. Alan Clephane's bravery and feats on the day had not gone unnoticed. King Robert the Bruce ushered him to his tent, and for his loss of hand the king offered the services of his best blacksmith, to create a hand of iron that could be fastened in place of the missing limb. And so this intricate device was invented.

Made of iron, the apparatus was designed to fasten to the elbow. The hand itself was fixed by screws to the frame. A lever in the hand could be pulled to clasp the fingers in a grasp which could hold the likes of a sword.

The Clephanes of Carslogie Castle were described as an "exceedingly tall race of men", proud and loyal to their Scottish kings. The last Clephane was Major-General William Douglas Clephane whose daughter married into the Northampton family in 1830. There were no more male heirs to claim Carslogie Castle and its estate.

Charles Douglas Compton was the third Marquis of Northampton. With the Clephane family name morphing into the Northampton family, they took the riches of the

Clephanes including the iron arm of Alan Clephane, which had been carefully looked after for five hundred years. The Northampton family kindly lent it out to be displayed at the Glasgow exhibition in 1888.

Clephane's iron arm.

I have the book that was brought out in 1890 highlighting the Glasgow exhibition's memorials. It's here that I found mention of the hand and a curious drawing. I decided to track down with devious cunning to get the actual phone number of the owners of Castle Ashby at their home residence in Warwickshire, the home of the 7th Marquis of Northampton – Spencer Compton. I hoped that the iron hand of Alan Clephane still existed and hadn't rusted its way out of existence.

When I phoned, unbelievably, Spencer Compton himself actually answered! I managed to swerve his first question of "How did you get this number?" by mentioning "I live near Carslogie Castle." In spite of his defensive reaction to a nuisance call, his curiosity was aroused, as he was the representative of this ancient proud family, and I was calling about something I am sure he doesn't get asked a lot these days. We had a leisurely and pleasant conversation on his ancient Scottish heritage. I was overjoyed to find the 7th Marquis of Northampton had indeed preserved the iron hand! It still existed, and his butler went to examine and photo the item for me.

It has never been photographed before and hasn't seen much exposure since the Glasgow exhibition in 1888. This is an item before its time, a wonderful example of a craftsman's work. I hope the 8th Marquis takes as great care of the item as his forbears have. To me it is a wonderful piece of history, and I am overjoyed to have tracked it down. I thank the Marquis of Northampton for letting me use his photos here to show.

And there's more...

I mentioned George R. R. Martin and his Game of Thrones series of books and hugely successful TV programme. George has admitted to getting his storylines direct from British history, and a lot of standout Scottish historic moments have been mirrored in the books and programme.

The programme highlights the North-South divide because of a massive ice wall which is patrolled by the "Night's Watch" to stop the undesirables getting over it...one can see this as a reference to the two Roman walls in Scotland: Hadrian's and the Antonine Wall. Another storyline the programme and books followed was the "Red Wedding" in which the "King of the North" and his followers were murdered at a dinner with their allied friends. This event has happened a few times with Scottish royalty, one occasion being in James II's Reign. In 1452 he had as guests for dinner at Stirling Castle the 8th Earl of Douglas and his brother. At the desired moment a bull's head was served (a symbol of death) and both earls were brutally murdered.

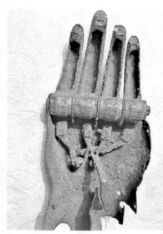

Details of Alan Clephane's iron hand.

Now we come to the significance of the iron hand. In the series of books and film, "Jaime Lannister" is the male heir to Westeros and in one incident has his hand severed when captured by his enemies. A brave swordsman himself, he has it replaced by a mechanical hand of gold! Of course, this mirrors the story of Alan Clephane from Carslogie Castle in Cupar.

It does seem George R. R. Martin has a good eye for Scottish history.

Further reading

Scottish National Memorials, ed. James Paton, 1890

Patrick Gordon's Bruce, reprinted 1718...original edition 1615 (from original manuscript 1369)

History of the County of Fife, by John M. Leighton, 1840 (Carslogie/Clephane family).

Chapter 2

The Hangover from Hell

Scotland in 1410 was chaos. In 1390 King Robert the Third had taken the throne. He was a troubled man, disabled from being injured in a horse accident in his youth, and a man not actually called Robert, but named John. The last "John" on the throne of Scotland had been John Balliol, a weak king who lost his throne. It was embarrassingly pulled from him by the English king Edward I, after which he was sent out of harm's way to live the rest of his life out in France, like a naughty boy spanked by his elders and sent to the spare room!

So a king named John would have brought back too many bad memories. It had become a cursed name in Scotland, while the name King Robert had prestige and honour from past holders of the title. Robert III it was to be, and crowned he was in 1390.

But his physical disabilities left him a weak king, and on his behalf his brother Robert Stewart the Duke of Albany would actually step forward and make the hard decisions in his brother's stead. Robert Stewart was the second son of King Robert II, he ran Falkland Palace as his headquarters and held the titles of Earl of Fife, Earl of Menteith, Earl of Buchan, Earl of Atholl, Earl of Mar and in 1398 Duke of Albany.

The Duke of Albany was a ruthless man: when his nephew David the Duke of Rothesay, heir to the throne of Scotland, went against his wishes and married the daughter of the Earl of Douglas, it was the final straw. He had no more tolerance of the young pup's constant undermining and interference with his plans for the country.

Prince David was captured by soldiers at St Andrews and banged up in the Falkland Palace dungeons, to be forgotten about as his uncle Albany repaired the political damage caused.

And forgotten David was. Weeks later he was eventually found in his basement cell of the palace starved to death; it was found he had eaten his own fingers in an attempt to survive.

King Robert III, terrified for his other son James, sent him on a ship to escape his uncle's power, with France as the destination, but pirates intercepted the ship and led the Scottish prince to the English king Henry IV in London. There Prince James would be held for the next eighteen years.

These events were too much for King Robert III.

There was an inquest in the Scottish Parliament concerning Prince David's death in 1402, but the jury was made up of Albany's supporters and friends. He was cleared of any wrongdoing. And after this verdict, the king deteriorated, till in 1406 he died and the title of king passed to his son James, who was sitting in an English prison. Following this unfortunate event, Robert Stewart, the Duke of Albany, could rule Scotland instead, as an unopposed custodian – and with an iron fist he did just that.

But for Albany, trouble was brewing on the west coast of Scotland, in the lands of the MacDonald's. The trouble was over titles and land. The male succession to the Earldom of Ross had become extinct, and the Lord of the Isles, Donald MacDonald, who was King Robert II's grandson, claimed both the title and the land on behalf of his wife, Margaret, Countess of Ross.

The Duke of Albany, the Governor of Scotland, refused to accept this claim and supported that of his own son. In this circumstance, the Lord of the Isles planted the flag of rebellion. With a newly made alliance with England, he received from Henry IV a fleet of ships for the use of his substantial army. At the head of 10,000 clansmen, fully armed with bows, pole axes and swords, he landed on the west coast and moved east with the intention of attacking the towns loyal to Albany, making Aberdeen his goal. En route, he met stiff resistance from the Black Angus, Angus Dubh Mackay of Farr, who stalled the army for a while. There was a small battle at Dingwall where he was captured, and Angus's brother Rory Gald was killed with his clan around him. MacDonald Lord of the Isles then moved his army towards Aberdeen with the news coming that Albany had an army moving north to intercept him.

The highland capital, Inverness, closed its walls against MacDonald Lord of the Isles and manned the town's defences. The Lord of the Isles, after the battle at Dingwall, needed supplies and food for his army and therefore sent a demand for money, clothes, and drink to the town chiefs, with the threat that if the request was not granted the town would be ransacked and destroyed in an orgy of violence. The Lord of the Isles left sufficient officers and men to deal with the matter, and they camped at the north side of the Kessock ferry, possibly as many as 500 men. If and when the demand for supplies was met, the goods were to be sent with the men to meet the main army heading towards Aberdeen and equip them with the provisions and supplies. The Inverness town chiefs met and thought things out…they were no stranger to the Lord of the Isles, he had looted the town before and taken nearby Urquhart Castle on the shore of Loch Ness in 1395 in a wave of violence.

There was every reason to be wary: they might meet the demands of the army, but there remained the worry that the returning army from whatever happened in Aberdeen would raid the town on the way back, seeing Inverness as a soft touch, because it would make perfect sense. With 10,000 men they needed a considerable amount of food and provisions to keep them happy.

So as MacDonald's islanders waited impatiently on the hillside for their demands to be met, the Inverness baillies came up with a cunning plan. Inverness had a few hundred men and citizens it could arm in defence of the town, a trained, obedient force, and along with such militia as they could drum up in defence of their own lands and liberty, they took an all or nothing approach to their own lives and those of their families who were facing the wrath of the MacDonald clansmen.

It was decided to send a note of submission to the MacDonalds on the hill but pleading that it would take a bit of time to gather the cattle and provisions of cheese and mutton and clothes they demanded. While the order was being made up, they did have vast quantities of whisky, barrels of which were listed in the demand. These the town had to hand and could be delivered straight away.

The MacDonalds were delighted at the offer of subjection from the Inverness town chiefs, and the whisky barrels were duly and humbly delivered.

A well-earned wee dram was taken from the first barrels, and the officers in command had a good drink. Then they offered it to all the other five hundred MacDonalds, who thought it was the spoils of war and no offence to drink a glass to their great Lord of the Isles. With the taste of success on their lips and night drawing near, fires were lit, and another barrel of whisky was cracked open to continue the celebration. Many glasses were raised again…then just another wee dram was had…and another…and then they must have noticed how thirsty this ransoming of Inverness actually was, so another cask was breached amid great cheers.

In July, the nights up here in the north of Scotland can be as light as day, with a setting sun that only just dips below the horizon by midnight before appearing again. Early July in 1411 would have been no different. The Inverness baillies opened the town gates a little after midnight, and a small armed battalion of Inverness gentry crept out and headed towards the north side of the Kessock ferry where the MacDonalds had made camp.

Under the now empty barrels of whisky, they saw a small felled forest of legs and kilts, men splayed out everywhere around the smouldering campfires, snoring loudly. Some men were still standing, and with enormous broad grins on their faces they welcomed the newcomers to the camp with incoherent songs and offers of drink! Whatever orders had been left for security and the postings of sentries had been lost in the drunken translations…the entire MacDonald forces were, to a man, so drunk they could barely stand.

The Inverness detachment attacked this shambles and put the very drunk MacDonalds to the sword! Every one. For the price of a few barrels of whisky, Inverness had been saved.

Over to the east from Inverness, the Lord of the Isles' army camped at Garioch, at a locality called Harlaw. Scouts had brought news that the Earl of Mar's army was near. It looked like the reckoning between the two forces would be settled there in the morning.

The Earl of Mar had marched from Aberdeen and found the waiting foes at the waters of the Urie (or Ury) near the junction with the River Don. Mar could see his army was outmatched in numbers, but in armour and training he thought himself superior to the clansmen arrayed against him. He decided the battle must be fought here and positioned his best knights in the vanguard under command of the Constable of Dundee and the Sheriff of Angus. Mar drew up the main strength of his army in the rear including Clan Murray, the Straitons, Maules, and Irvings. The Lesley, Lovel, and Stirling families were there also with the clan chiefs, and Mar placed himself at the head of this body of men.

MacDonald Lord of the Isles had his Mackintoshes and MacLeans, with other highland chiefs, as the first line, with the mass of MacDonald strength behind. They cried their battle chants, and this ragged line of tartan steel broke into a charge upon their enemy. But the lowland knights met them with firmness and bravery, with spears levelled and battle-axes smiting downwards from iron-clad war horses. The more lightly armoured clansmen fell in heaps as their boiled-leather chest armour and shields were split apart, no match for iron plate. But over their dead the Highlanders kept coming, pulling down a knight here and there, with numbers thinning. The Constable of Dundee, Sir James Scrymegeour, fell with many of his men around him, pulled from his horse and finished by a highland dirk. Knights were led forward to address the balance and highland heads and targes were split as more clansmen fell on the field. But still the Highlanders kept coming. The Earl of Mar then led forward his main forces and split the Highlanders, taking the fight right in amongst the thick ranks of his enemies, his own forces suffering casualties but the Highlanders more.

The vanguard was no more – Sir Alexander Ogilvy, the Sheriff of Angus, with his eldest son George Ogilvy were cut down in this sea of steel. This was a sore casualty list. Sir Thomas Murray, Sir Robert Maule, Sir Alexander Irving, Sir William Abernethy, Sir Alexander Straiton, James Lovell, Alexander of Stirling, Irving of Drum, and Sir Robert Davidson with the Provost of Aberdeen and his 500 men were all among the Duke of Albany's slain.

The Highlanders left 900 dead on the field, including the Chiefs of MacLean and Mackintosh with Hector Rufus their Lieutenant-General under Clan Ross. The terrible battle was fought on the 24th of July 1411. Ballads were written about the battle, and songs and laments were sung. Mar held the ground with his battle-scarred men, expecting the battle to renew in the morning. But by morning the Highlanders had retreated towards Inverurie, having looted Mar's baggage train. This was a tactical victory of sorts for Mar, still holding the ground in the morning, but his losses may have seemed like a defeat to him.

On the north east side of the river Urie, at a place called Legget's Den, is a tomb with four large stones, covered with broad stone above. This was the tomb of the two highland chiefs MacLean and Mackintosh. But it was moved in 1815, and only one of the stones remains, as part of an embankment built to prevent the Urie river flooding.

The Battle of Harlaw was a desperate affair with both sides fought to a standstill, a drawn battle of sorts. Lord McDonald and his supporters went back to the isles and the following year he submitted to the authority of Albany.

What we must imagine is how the Lord of the Isles would have fared with another 500 men and provisions, how history could have changed had he not demanded the barrels of whisky from the Inverness chiefs.

Further reading

Battle of Harlaw...Scottish Battlefields...Chris Brown

Inverness Session records...Gazetteer of Scotland...R Chambers 1844

Chapter 3

Scotland's Peculiar Children

In the research I do for my stories, it often has me nose deep in fabulously rare books, first editions dating as far back as 1560 giving the details of history just passed, written as fresh as when it happened.

These books now have been written and rewritten by authors following one another through the centuries until the original history has been warped into a fair bit of untruth. One writer slightly changes the tale, and the next writer steals the same story and adds his tuppence worth, and so on until we have a mangled story showing new readers not much in the way of historical facts. It is my pleasure to read the original source books and dictate the history as it was written, and of course to credit the writer.

Many mainstream history authors were a credit to themselves, writing one big volume of a book for absolutely no benefit other than their own interests. Much history is recalled simply because a character of notable title wanted his achievements kept to make future sires of his house proud.

But it is not until the year 1800 that printing presses were readily available in Scotland, and it is a sad fact that we as a nation were one of the last in Europe to adopt the printing press, and start the mass production of books. The old tomes that had been written and treasured in single volumes were brought forward out of secret dusty attics and finally produced in numbers upon the printing press. History could be accessed by all.

My interest is in diaries written by less important figures, that give a view of the time period, of its struggles and daily life. And it is in such books that I find the gems such as the one that I give you in this chapter...about the peculiar children of Scotland.

A little to the north of the village of Largo in Fife where I was born, there lies a forest within a deep valley. It is not generally known where it got its name, but in my lifetime, it has always been known as "Kiel's Den". It is a beautiful place much regaled by dog walkers and nature lovers. If we follow the river upstream we come to the ruined castle and farm of Pitscottie, the ancient seat of the Lindsay family where the historian Robert Lindsay wrote his book *The History and Chronicles of Scotland 1436-1565*. I hold a 1778 copy in my library, and it is in this book that we find a most strange case.

There is to the west side of Scotland, in Galloway, the legend of a cannibal family that terrorised the area in the reign of James I.[*] They were named the "Sawney Bean Family". According to legend, Sawney Bean eloped with a woman and eked out an existence living in the dark reaches of a cave by the sea. There they raised a large family, and they subsisted by attacking strangers and feeding on their flesh! The story goes they were eventually hunted down by King James and the miserable wretches were dragged

---

[*] Reigned 1406–1437: James was the younger brother of David who was starved to death by his cruel uncle Robert Duke of Albany, see Chapter 2.

from their cave, taken to Edinburgh where the women were burnt and the men hacked to pieces...there were over a dozen of them.

The story itself has, in fact, no history to verify the gory tale, and the earliest accounts of it appear in a broadsheet newspaper sold on the streets of London in 1724, written by a Captain Charles Johnston. He writes the story as a factual piece, but nothing in today's history can back up the tale, even though the cave where Sawney and his family supposedly lived does actually exist on the Galloway coastline.

But was Captain Charles Johnston taking liberties with Scottish history? In Pitscottie's book in the year 1460 he makes an interesting note about an incident in Angus, which does remind the reader a little of the Sawney Bean story. I will quote it in full...

> About this time there was apprehended and taken for an abominable and cruel abuse a brigand who haunted and dwelled with his whole family and household out of all men's company in a place of Angus called Feindes den. This mischievous man had an execrable fashion to take all young men and children that either he could steal quietly or take away by any means without the knowledge of the people and bring them and eat them and the more young they were he held them the more tender and greater delicate. For which damnable and cursed abuse he with his wife, bairns and family were all burnt except one young lass of one year old which was saved and brought to Dundee where she was

fostered and brought up. But when she came to the age of a woman's years she was condemned and burnt quick for the same crime (her father was convicted). It is said that when this young woman was commanded forth to the place of execution that there gathered an innumerable multitude of people about her and specially of women cursing and worrying that she was so unhappy to commit so damnable deeds, to whom she turned about with a mad and furious countenance, saying, 'wherefore chide ye with me as I had committed an unworthy act. Give me credit and trust me, if ye had experience of eating of women and men's flesh ye would think the same so delicious that ye would never forbear it again,' and so with an obstinate mind this unhappy creature without sign or outward token of repentance died in the sight of the whole people for her misdeeds that she was adjudged to.

You can see where the writer of the Sawney Bean tale may have got inspiration from, in the same manner as Daniel Defoe got his source material for his book *Robinson Crusoe* from the true story of the Largo seaman Alexander Selkirk's stay on San Fernandez island. From my knowledge of witch trials in Scotland, the method of burning a victim at the stake would have the condemned strangled with a rope first ("wirreit" as the old Scots records put it) before the fire was lit to consume the body.

But in some cases the witch was greatly hated and

the fury of the crowd was enormous. The witch in some trial records is described as "brunt quick" which means that the flames were left to do the job without the usual strangulation! She was not strangled and therefore was suffered to be burnt alive. Her screams were for all to hear!

This may give us an idea of the fury of the Dundee crowd, and to me makes the whole thing a bit more believable.

The reference to Feindes Den leads me to look at the area of Denfind: the lands are included as belonging to the Barony of Downie. And it is here when looking in *Castles of Scotland*, by Martin Coventry, that I can learn that the baron's actual castle doesn't exist anymore. The stone was used for other more modern building projects, and all that remains is a small rectangular doocot near the Downie Mill. But what is interesting is that the castle owners are noted as being the Lindsay family, the same family as that of the author of the original story, written by Robert Lindsay of Pitscottie, who died in 1580.

I feel Robert would have had knowledge of the facts of this story from his family history, albeit when writing about it in 1570, over a hundred years after when it happened in 1460.

I visited the Denfind area in 2018 looking for the area where the cannibals lived and hunted their victims. After a long search I found the area covered by flat farm fields supported by a dense forest that dipped sharply into a tight valley. Pitscottie called this valley "Feindes Den" and over the years it has changed to "Denfind". We have the area they were famed to live in, and also a small cave hidden as a three-metre-deep recess, high enough to stand in. It is on the map as "Cat's Cave"...also known as "Ghoul's Cave" and I can see how history has embedded itself into the landscape with the gory family's exploits.

The cave was a brilliant hideout – it is impossible to see from the pathway and a nightmare to reach through heavy undergrowth and steep ravines. This was perfect for attacking victims on the forest path: they could drag them down to this cave location and then butcher them! Thinking of the name "Cat's Cave", I wonder if the child that survived the original burning of her parents and siblings was called Catherine?

In James IV's reign,* the king brought the renaissance to Scotland in a wave of prosperity and foreign trade. He was a thinker and loved the arts, and it is to his exploration of the peculiar, we go to next.

This new tale again comes from Pitscottie's *History of Scotland* book. The story involves the isolated island in the Firth of Forth, Inchkeith.

The island sits just east of today's Forth bridges. The island today has no population, but it was fought over in the past by the Vikings and later the English. All that remains of its bloody history is a ruined Augustinian abbey on the 22 acres of the island. But its solitude seemed perfect for King James IV of Scotland with his curious mind. In 1488 he had his court find a woman who had been born with a speech defect: she was completely dumb but otherwise healthy and young. The curious King thought

---

* Reigned 1488-1513

to place this woman on the island of Inchkeith and would have her want for nothing. Food, clothes, and books were to be deposited for her use. Her only task was to bring up two young orphan bairns over the years in the solitude of the island. The whole concept of the experiment was to look at the children after so many years in nothing but the company of a mother who could not naturally speak! The question was…what language, if any, would the young children eventually learn?

According to Robert Lindsay, the result was, some said, that they spoke good Hebrew, but he added that he did not himself know this.

Another of James's curiosities was a male child, which had two bodies from the waist up. Its two backs fastened to each other. The king made it his new project to protect these conjoined twins and make sure they wanted for nothing. Pitscottie wrote about how musical instruments were introduced to them, and "they became in short time very ingenious and cunning in the art of music whereby they could play and sing two parts, the one the treble, the other the tenor, which was very douce and melodious to hear by the common people, who treated them wondrous well. Also they could speak sundry and diverse languages, that is to say Latin, French, Italian, Spanish, Dutch, Danish and English and Irish."

The sad inevitability was that one brother died. The surviving brother, naturally horrified, was recorded by Pitscottie as saying…

> How can I be merry, that has my true marrow
> as a dead carrion upon my back, which was wont

to sing and play with me, to commune and talk in like manner. When I was sad, he would give me comfort, and I would do likewise to him. But now I have nothing but dolour of the bearing of so heavy a burden, dead and cold, undissolved on my back, which takes all earthly pleasure from me in this present life. Therefore I pray to almighty God, to deliver me out of this present life, that we may be laid and dissolved in the earth where from we came.

And so not long after this last request the second twin died also.

Chapter 4

The Bothwell Blues

The mid-16th century was a precarious time to live in Scotland – in the realm of Mary Queen of Scots. Previous to her coming of age, several regents had ruled the land in her name, all running the country like 1920s Chicago gangsters, one offing the other in spates of assassinations and murders. With religious turmoil, invasion from England, thousands of French troops engaged against the English in Scotland, and the dagger and pistol of the assassin to cope with, it is fair to say that life was very cheap!

It is against this background that James Hepburn, the fourth Earl of Bothwell, steps into the history books as he plays his part in the tragic life of Mary Queen of Scots.

Bothwell came from a border family and was born in 1536 in the mighty fortress of Crichton Castle. As a border lord he would be used to the invasions from and wars with England. His family held the hereditary position of Lord Admiral of Scotland, and James Hepburn took the position from his father in 1556.

James had supported Mary's French mother Mary of Guise when she was Regent of Scotland after King James V's death and transferred his devotion and loyalty from her to Mary.

In 1561, he took the Scottish fleet to France, picked up the Scottish queen and delivered her safely to Leith on the 19th of August. But the euphoria on the arrival of the new queen was soon shattered. When news came that a priest was now celebrating Mass with her in newly protestant Scotland, there was uproar and riots took place in Edinburgh. However, her half-brother had agreed she could practise her own faith...in private.

In 1565 the Queen married Henry Stewart, Lord Darnley, a handsome, tall fellow, who it seemed was equal to the Queen in his love of sports, hunting and music. Like Mary he was a great-grandson of Henry VII of England, both of them having Tudor and Stewart blood.

But the marriage went against the wishes of all her advisers: it did not affect her popularity but made her enemies among those close to her. Darnley was the son of the Earl of Lennox. The family of Lennox had sided with the English in Henry VIII's 'rough wooing' in 1544–49: grand abbeys and towns were burnt out in a fury because Queen Mary's regents refused to marry her off in a union with King Henry's son. King Henry's forces attacked by both land and sea. Much of the eastern Scottish coastline was taken by surprise and battered by the unopposed English navy. At the same time, an English mounted army crossed the border and destroyed every township it came upon, until part of the English force was attacked and beaten by the Scots at Ancrum Moor in 1545. Darnley's family had been pardoned as late as September 1654 for their part in supporting the 'rough wooing'. Once married to Queen Mary, Lord Darnley behaved in an oafish manner, belittling the Queen in public and preferring to go whoring secretly in the back streets of Edinburgh with his base friends rather than take up his court duties. Mary was six months pregnant when her secretary David Rizzio was set upon by a mob of retainers and murdered in front of Mary in Holyroodhouse in 1566. He was rumoured to be a Catholic agent sent by the Pope. Lord Darnley was easily convinced, disliking the man who was such a favourite of Mary's. Darnley led the assault...Rizzio was stabbed fifty times and significantly Darnley's dagger was left in the man's dying body.

The marriage broke down because of this act. Early in 1567, Lord Darnley had taken himself to bed, ill from what was thought to be syphilis. He was deliberately kept from the new royal baby lest he infect him also, and so lodged in part of the Provost of Edinburgh's house, called Kirk o Field.

On the 10th of February at 2 am, the Provost's house exploded, lighting up a dark Edinburgh sky in a sheet of bright light for a few moments, as death and destruction rained down on the city. The cellar had been crammed full of gunpowder, the work of an assassin, but Queen Mary herself had led the ill Lord Darnley to this building. Worse news came...Lord Darnley's body had been found unmarked from the explosion, but it seems he had been strangled along with his servant!

At this time James Hepburn, Lord Bothwell, had been in very close contact with Mary and the murders were now being laid at his door by supporters of Lord Darnley. A trial in the Privy Council was held where Bothwell was accused of the murder, but this trial was arranged and set up by himself. The court was filled with his own men and retainers, and no real accuser was let in. Bothwell was therefore acquitted in the farcical trial. It did him no favours with his growing enemies.

Lord Bothwell now put his army around Mary's person and again showed his loyalty to her. But behind the scenes he was plotting his own future, with one eye on the crown of Scotland. A meeting was arranged: twenty-nine lords of Parliament were to attend a back-street tavern in the Canongate area of Edinburgh. There they were all to sign a bond endorsing Bothwell to be fit and trusted enough to wed the newly widowed Queen, and all were to state that they favoured the act.

Bothwell showed the bond to Mary, who refused the offer on the grounds that there was too much scandal about her husband's death (that and the fact Bothwell was six inches shorter than Mary). Bothwell decided to take matters into his own hands. On 21 April, the Queen was seized by Bothwell and eight hundred men-at-arms and "guided" to Dunbar castle, supposedly for her safety. The Queen was simply abducted, and in some reports raped by Bothwell! She stayed at the castle for two weeks while her divorce was arranged by Bothwell. On the 15th of May, they were married.

The nobles at once rebelled at the news, with Queen Mary's stepbrother now joining those taking up arms against Bothwell. Not having sufficient strength to give battle, Bothwell fled. He was chased to the islands of Orkney, from where he took a ship to Norway.

There he encountered kinsmen of Anna Throndsen. In a strange twist, she had been Bothwell's first – discarded – wife. He was arrested and thrown into a Danish fortress of

Dragsholm in Zealand. He would linger in a jail for the next eleven years. Chained and gangrenous, he died a screaming madman in 1573.

The next chapter of Bothwell's story makes eerie reading...for a while his body was left to rot, unburied and forgotten in the castle dungeons. After some time, the sea air started to preserve the corpse of Bothwell. It became a showpiece to visitors to the castle. Then painters started to etch and draw its likeness, a curiosity of mummified Scottish royalty in the tragedy of the life of Mary Queen of Scots. It was moved to Faarevejle church and placed in a glass container, where again it became a curiosity for the next three centuries. Bothwell's cadaver was eventually buried in 1976 in an oak coffin.

Bothwell was an over-ambitious man, who reduced to tatters what dignity Queen Mary had left after the death of her husband Lord Darnley. Those who remained loyal mustered to her and were defeated in a battle at Langside against her stepbrother James Stuart. Mary fled to England,

Bothwell's body at Faarevejle church in Denmark.

where she was held and eventually beheaded by her cousin, Queen Elizabeth of England.

What remains of Bothwell today are the picture so delicately painted of him when he was a lord, showing him in all his grace and standing...and the picture of his mummified corpse drawn a hundred years after his death.

Portrait of James, Earl of Bothwell from the Mary Queen of Scots Centre

Painting of Bothwell's corpse from the National Gallery of Scotland.

Chapter 5

The Anstruther Pirate Hunters

During the troubled reign of Mary Queen of Scots, in her youth and again after her forced abdication, a set of leaders were chosen to govern Scotland in her stead. Called "Regents", they carried out appointments in the name of the Queen in her infancy and in the name of her son James after her abdication.

James Stewart (born 1531) was a sibling of James V as was Mary (born 1542). But he was the offspring of one of the king's mistresses (the king had no less than five children by other women), a bastard son, and he was halfbrother to Mary. He was a wise man who supported the change in religion which resulted in the Reformation, and he defended Scottish interests manfully in battle. The battles of St Monans in 1548, Corrichie in 1562, and Langside in 1567 were won with him leading the army.

The unusual story told in this chapter is that James Stewart (titled the Earl of Moray) is on record as being in St Andrews as Regent in July 1568, to oversee the execution of Alexander Macker, a pirate who had been terrorising the coastline. He and six surviving pirate shipmates were taken to the beach, where they were trussed up and thrown into a deep fissure called the "Witchpool" in which they had been sentenced to drown for their crimes.

The sentence of drowning was rare in Scotland's courts. It was reserved for the worst of bestial crimes by those such as James Mitchel, who was convicted of bestality and drowned in Edinburgh's Nor Loch in March 1675.

There were only a handful of instances on record of "swimming a Witch" in Scotland (if she floated in the water she was deemed guilty, to sink and drown – innocent!) although some poems by David Vader and mob action in Pittenweem 1705 accounted for witch drownings. It was a death reserved for pirates and the above action has a relevance in this tale.

Anstruther in 1587 had a fortified harbour protecting the best fleet on Scotland's East coast. These ships traded with the continent and England in wool, coal, and fish. As if it was not already hard enough to navigate these waters, the captains of Anstruther's ships had the added misfortune of having their trade routes plagued by pirates.

Merchant ships laden with goods from the continent were regularly attacked as they came in to the home ports in Fife.

In 1587 a one-mast ship (known as a creer) turned into Anstruther harbour. They had been attacked by English pirates in the German Ocean (as the North Sea was known before the First World War) and their goods had all been ransacked and stolen. The crew was badly mauled, and the ship's captain, a fine respected figure in Anstruther, had been shot dead for his resistance to the English pirates.

Fury was aroused because they had been attacked just a few miles from the safety of their own harbour and its guns. Even while the complaint was being addressed, another homeward-bound ship was also attacked by the same pirate vessel, now recognised to be under the command of the English pirate Thomas Hall.

There was an immediate council meeting with all four town baillies. It was decided to raise 1,000 merks* to rig out a mercenary ship in warlike manner to go after the English pirate and seek vengeance for the hurt so badly done to them. A warship meeting their approval was found docked in St Andrews harbour. Its old captain, Allan Lentrone, took the purse and set sail immediately. They knew the pirates were from southern England. So they set sail, with plans to linger at sea in the English Channel till the pirate ship could be identified.

The Anstruther town chiefs also contributed a small ship of their own, funded and sailed by Baillie William Anderson, with his son as part of the crew. It was to shadow the larger warship manned by Captain Lentrone and assist where needed.

On the three-day voyage towards the southern coast of England, passing trading vessels were stopped and interrogated for information and news of any sighting of Thomas Hall's band of pirates. One such large merchant vessel refused to stop at the requests of Captain Lentrone, and raised sails to avoid contact. Thinking they had found the guilty band of murderous thieves, the forward gun on the Scots warship responded by blasting the ship's mainsail down, rendering her defenceless. They then boarded her, but found nothing suspicious when the ship's captain

* The Anstruther Baillie William Anderson raised 1,000 merks!...the merk was a pre-Union Scots currency. It was two thirds of a Scots pound, making the money raised for the warship £750 Scots (a merk was worth one English shilling).

yielded to the boarding party. It was found to be nothing but a nervous trading ship, but what did come out of this skirmish was that the English trading ship did know of the pirate vessel the Scots were after – and could give its home port as being in Suffolk.

Towards Suffolk, then, the ship turned. It was there that Captain Lentrone prepared his men in arms for a deadly confrontation with the pirates. And they found them – sitting off the coast with spoil from a freshly attacked ship. As they cruised closer they recognized the stricken ship! It was another one from Anstruther harbour, taken as a prize by the pirates, and was being pulled to their home port in Suffolk. At the sight of the big Scots warship bearing down on them, the pirates turned their ship towards the coast and beached their own ship on the rocks as they tried to escape. A heavily-armed Scots landing party quickly made after them and caught them. But the alarm had gone through Suffolk at the invasion of warlike men advancing on the beach.

At this time relations were strained between England and Spain. An invasion force was expected. When the English approached the Scots, they were well prepared to defend themselves and thought the Spanish had landed, but Captain Lentrone and the Anstruther Baillie William Anderson explained their mission, which their bewildered hosts accepted – handing over the surviving pirates from Captain Thomas Hall's crew. Pirate captain Thomas Hall and five crew members were trussed up and put in the hold of the Scottish warship. Gifts and pleasantries were shared with the townsfolk of Suffolk for their understanding and help as the Scottish ships turned and made for home.

The two Scottish ships parted ways as they neared Fife. The warship returned to St Andrews with four of the pirates. The little boat manned by Baillie William Anderson pulled into the harbour of Anstruther to a hero's welcome. The whole town of five hundred people had come out to see the return. Baillie Anderson had the pirate captain Thomas Hall and a shipmate in crime displayed to the crowd. Then without the formality of a trial, ropes were put around their necks and tied to the harbour mooring posts. They were pushed off the end of the pier and the six-metre drop made sure Thomas Hall would never raid another Anstruther ship again. Justice had been done.

The fate of the four other pirate prisoners taken to St Andrews by Captain Lentrone is on record as "executed"!

With the pirates drowned in 1568 as witnessed by the Regent James Stewart himself, the 1587 pirates from Suffolk could expect nothing but a watery grave, with the "Witchpool" being used again.

In the St Andrews Kirk Session Records for May 1588, we can read of a request being made to Dave Watson the Dean of Guild (a carpenter) "to make a beir to burie the dead". With a period in jail to make an example of the English pirates first, this may be their bodies being issued to the ground as burial.

In Anstruther Churchyard by the middle of the east gable end of the parish kirk, there is a stone that represents the grave of the Anstruther skipper Captain Anderson.

It is interesting to note that along the Fife coast we find

the sea town of Buckhaven. It gained its name in the 15th century from pirates who were chased from English waters and settled here on the coast. It was known as Buccaneers' Haven...that name carries on today as Buckhaven.

Further reading

Anstruther, or Illustrations of Scottish Burgh Life, by George Gourley, Cupar 1888

Auld Anster, by Alison Thirkell, Anstruther 1976 (Buckie House) St Andrews Kirk Session Register, 1559-1600 (transcribed 1889, Scottish History Society)

Prisons and Punishment in Scotland, by Joy Cameron, Edinburgh 1983 (Canongate)

Chapter 6

One in the Eye for Roderick...in Skye

In the autumn of 2015, I found myself exploring the sounds of Skye and Sleat, the old haunts of the MacLeods, where the lament of sadness hangs over the near empty valleys and windswept moors where many a Highland village used to stand.

Once they had been ruled and protected by the clan chieftains – over hundreds of years. The clan would suffer the losses and share the spoils together. In heated exchanges of loyalties, they were bound to the chieftain and his personal decisions, in trivial disputes and royal commands.

Loyalty and pride carried men to fight for causes that were often ill-advised, with terrible consequences for the losers. Uprooting and banishment for many, as clan chiefs were replaced by others more loyal and more obedient to the monarch's causes.

The clan chiefs held legal power over their clansmen, and disobedience could mean languishing in cold castle dungeons for long stretches or even a sentence of death.

The traditional method of gathering your clansmen in strength to wage war was to bind a wooden cross together, covering it in the gore of an animal's blood and then with as much noise as possible to ride it through the villages and homesteads of the clansmen.

Once this "fiery cross" was observed, the clansmen

would grab weapons in haste and appear in strength at the gathering hotspot. The "fiery cross" would be passed from rider to rider through the glens till all had news of it. And then at the gathering place the reasons for launching the cross's journey would be explained, and plans for battle debated. To ignore the call of the "fiery cross" would result in death to those foolish enough. This was the power chiefs wielded over their men.

To raid, or be raided! This became the custom after the crops were harvested and gathered. Many clans had the reputation of being master cattle rustlers. Raiding and stealing their enemy's beasts might be enough to subdue the reason for wielding the fiery cross through the glens. Many clan chiefs had disputes that had lasted for decades after the original insult or grievance took place. Father to son carried the ill blood against their chosen enemy. They were a proud race of people where reputations meant everything to them. In 1601 on the Sleat peninsula, on the west coast island of Skye, a clan feud was to erupt in the MacDonalds' homeland.

It was nothing unusual to bond the clans with marriage, a peaceful agreement that would give further security in numbers and ships for both parties, if ever they were threatened by warlike others. While previously the clan chief could send his "fiery cross" across the land and gather maybe 400 sword-wielding men, a marriage union could now bring the total to over a thousand. This was power indeed!

This was the case in the summer of 1601: Domhnull Gorm Mor MacDonald of Sleat was to be married to the sister of Sir Roderick MacLeod, the chief who lived in the mighty Dunvegan Castle in Skye.

A happy occasion, you would have thought, and being neighbours the union of alliance would be fruitful for both clans. Sir Roderick sent his sister to his rival with a suitable dowry and pages to represent the upcoming union. Everything was ready for a glorious wedding and a joyous day for everyone involved. The bride was set to meet her intended husband on arrival at Sleat, but from this first meeting it was obvious that something was amiss, and that the sister of Sir Roderick MacLeod never met the high expectations of the chief of the MacDonalds.

What pleasantries were swapped between the two parties has never been disclosed, but actions in this case say more than words could ever do! Sir Roderick MacLeod's sister Margaret, the intended bride, had the misfortune of having her beautiful looks spoiled somewhat...by having only one eye!

Dunvegan Castle was an impressive retreat, it was built in the 14th century but the MacLeods had been there since 1270, descended from Viking stock and warriors of past battles including Bannockburn 1314 and Harlaw 1411. It was home to the famous Fairy Flag! This was a flag with mythical powers, only brought on to battlefields to procure a victory and it was draped over the marriage beds to make the marriages fruitful. It was a powerful talisman. But in this instance the flag's powers were never needed...

A Highland servant disturbed Sir Rory's solitude and rest, with news of riders approaching the grand Dunvegan Castle. He took himself down to the castle gates to see his uninvited guests and found a curious situation: it was his own sister! She had been returned.

But more curious thoughts prevailed him when he viewed her fellow travelling companions. She had made her journey, sent back from Sleat and MacDonald territory with...a one-eyed pageboy, a one-eyed West Highland terrier dog, and his one-eyed sister Janet was sitting on a one-eyed horse!

There was no forward message from the MacDonald chief, just MacLeod's sister returned with the collection of unhappy one-eyed creatures! The insult needed no words, and this rejection brought fury from Sir Rory MacLeod. MacDonald's rash comic performance brought the fiery cross out and through the homesteads of the Macleod clan. War was declared on the MacDonald's of Sleat! Sir Rory Macleod thought he had time before the MacDonalds would respond to his declaration and went to the Campbell lands to seek an alliance with the age-old MacDonald enemies. While he was gone from Dunvegan Castle he left the clan in charge of his brother Alexander.

But the MacDonalds were swift to arm and invade the Macleod lands. Alexander MacLeod had to gather his men, and they met the tartan hordes from Sleat just under the Cuillin hills in Skye. It was an engagement that would be named "the battle of Benquhillan". It lasted a full day's fighting, till only Alexander and thirty of his MacLeod men survived the slaughter and surrendered the field to the MacDonalds. An insult over an unglamorous sister had just cost hundreds of men's lives.

A historic footnote to the results of the battle, written

at Stirling Castle 22nd August 1601, was that the government Privy Council demanded that MacLeod and MacDonald be observed to hold the King's peace. MacLeod was to repair to the lands of the Earl of Argyle and MacDonald to the Marquis of Huntly within six days of receiving the order – or be accused of treason, whereupon the Council would sort out the disagreement!

Sir Roderick Macleod would eventually find happiness in marriage with the sister of Kenneth Mackenzie of Kintail who – I'm sure – had lovely eyes!

Chapter 7

The Duel to the Death

As I sit in my garden and relax in the sunshine with a beer, my rare breed hens are scuffing about the garden beside me. Scottish Dumpie hens have a history going all the way back to AD 900, when Scottish armies used them scattered around the force's baggage area – any enemies creeping near at night would set the hens off and alarm the Scots into action. They provided meat, eggs, and good sentries, which were invaluable qualities for the Scottish army. I have two cockerels, proud defensive creatures, who on occasion will go head to head in bloody dispute, feathers raised and face to face. A violent fury erupts as they brawl, but noble highs to the winner and loser: one will back down, giving the winner crowing rights. Then peace settles and they are back to scuffing about in the garden again.

Our next chapter has two proud cockerels in human form, fighting in their own duel to the death. As the Scottish Dumpies have their code of honour, so did these men, and their pride nearly cost both of them their lives.

The year is 1613. The first of our fiery combatants was Edward, 2nd Lord Bruce of Kinloss, son of Lord George Bruce of Culross, who erected and built Culross Abbey in 1608, reaping the reward of seeing it finally finished, but dying two years later, leaving a wealthy legacy of Culross Palace and a lucrative coal mine and salt works to his son Edward.

The other was Sir Edward Sackville, the 4th Earl of Dorset, born in 1591. He was an English courtier, soldier and politician, the son of Robert Sackville, 2nd Earl of Dorset.

Edward Bruce had been born in Hardwick, Derbyshire in 1597, one of five siblings in the Bruce family. He had close ties to King James VI and I, who was a family friend, and who bestowed the Order of the Bath on Edward in 1610. It was an honourable order of chivalry to be appointed to as a knight.

But a problem developed at a society gathering at the Earl of Derby's mansion where the finery of England drank brandy and raised glasses in toasts to King James. Some say that among the ladies present was the granddaughter of the Earl of Derby, Venetia Stanley, in her fine ballgown, who flirted dangerously with the young men, two of whom held her special attention...the two young Edwards: nineteen-year-old Edward Bruce and twenty-two-year-old Edward Sackville.

Whatever the truth of it, blows followed insults and then a glove was produced and thrown down in a gesture that meant that the way to settle the argument was a duel, with swords or pistols! It was certainly a foolhardy thing to do in public: each man now was committed to dealing with the matter as gentlemen.

But with the argument being so public, news reached the ears of society and men of power, with the elders of both families – not to mention King James VI and I – frowning on the action. But the two aggrieved men, much motivated by pride, decided to carry the duel on outside of the British Isles. It would be settled properly as gentlemen, with rapier duelling swords. Men would be chosen as seconds, to take up the fight if need be, and there would be a surgeon for each camp. The battle would take place in Holland.

A letter offering the challenge from Bruce to Sackville was hand-delivered by a Scottish friend to Lord Sackville in his father-in-law's mansion in Derbyshire. (So he was already married!)

Lord Bruce wrote from France saying that he was confident that Lord Sackville's honour gave Sackville the same courage to do him right, that it did to do him wrong. Bruce offered his opponent the choice of weapons, time and place. "By doing this," he wrote, "you shall shorten revenge, and clear the idle opinion the world hath of our honours."

Sackville replied that he did not seek a quarrel but was always ready to meet any who desired to make trial of his valour, and would specify time, place and weapon within a month. "In the meantime be as secret of the appointment, as it seems you be desirous of it."

On the 10th of August 1613, Sackville wrote to Bruce: "I am ready at Ter Goes a town in Zeeland, to give you that satisfaction your sword can render you" and said that he would not specify a particular day but desired Bruce "to make a definite and speedy repair for your own honour, and fear of prevention".

Bruce's reply: "I have received your letter by your man, and acknowledge you have honourably dealt with me and now I come with all possible haste to meet you."

What happened was described by the one duellist to survive, Edward Sackville. He was trying to justify his actions, so we have to take all he says with a pinch of salt. According to Sackville, it was agreed that they should go via Antwerp to Bergen-op-Zoom where only a village divided the Dutch Republic's territories from those of the Habsburgs, so that after the duel "he that could might presently exempt himself from the justice of the country".

In the pre-duel negotiations, Lord Bruce told Sackville's second that he wished to fight Sackville alone, without a second, because so worthy a gentleman and a friend could not stand by and see him do what he had to do to satisfy himself and his honour. Sackville's second protested "that such intentions were bloody and butcherly, far unfitting a noble personage who should desire to bleed for reputation not for life". According to Sackville, Bruce's intentions made him "verily mad with anger the Lord Bruce should thirst after my life with a kind of assuredness, seeing I had come so far, and needlessly to give him leave to regain his lost reputation".

The parties having arrived at the place agreed on, alighted from their horses and made preparations for the onset.

The locality was a meadow ankle deep in water and there the two men stripped to their shirts and began the fatal encounter. Sackville having become very excited, was threatened for a time of being worsted, and he received several severe thrusts from Lord Bruce's sword until the weapons of each became entangled, a mutual release was proposed, this was declined by both, the victory looked to go with whoever could make his opponent let go. Lord Sackville by a violent effort succeeded in freeing his own weapon, whilst he still retained hold of Lord Bruce's sword, at whose throat he now made a lunge and called on him to ask his life and yield his sword. The demand was refused and Sackville passed his sword through the young nobleman but missed his heart. He pulled his sword out and passed it through Bruce's body at another place, upon which Bruce exclaimed, "Oh I am slain!" but endeavoured with all his strength to trip up and overturn his antagonist. But this was only the last effort of despair, and Lord Bruce was immediately prostrate on the ground. Sackville once again asked if he would yield, to which Bruce replied with defiant scorn.

At this point Lord Bruce's surgeon, who had remained at a distance, exclaimed that he would die if his wound were not stopped. Lord Sackville inquired whether his antagonist wished now to have medical attendance, to which Lord Bruce gave faint consent.

Sackville retired to his surgeon in whose arms he remained a while for want of blood – with "strong waters" and his surgeon's diligence, he quickly recovered. According to Sackville, he now "escaped a great danger, for my Lord's surgeon, when nobody dreamt of it, ran at me with his Lord's sword. Had not mine with my sword interposed himself, I had been by those base hands slain. Although the Lord Bruce, weltering in his own blood, and past expectation of life, conformable to all his former carriage, was undoubtedly noble, cried out, 'Rascal, hold thy hand!'" And so Edward Bruce, Lord of Kinloss died.

Silver casket holding Edward Bruce's heart.

The body of Lord Bruce was deposited in the church of Bergen-op-Zoom and a monument was erected to his memory, which was destroyed in the siege of the town in 1747. His heart was embalmed and taken to the family vault in Culross next to the Abbey church of Culross. In 1808, the estate passed to Sir Robert Preston who thinking the story nothing but legend searched for the heart and found it, encased in a silver case. Drawings were taken of it and it was reburied in the crypt. His title was taken by his younger brother Thomas Bruce, who would become 1st Earl of Elgin.

Lord Sackville, although the victor of the duel, was close to death himself, he had been run through the chest by Bruce, and several other wounds required attention, including a severed finger resulting from that last desperate grapple with each other's swords. It took months for him to recover, but recover he did and made his way back to England and the prize of Venetia Stanley.

According to the gossipy and unreliable John Aubrey, as recounted in his *Brief Lives*, "Sir Kenelm Digby married that celebrated beauty and courtesan, Mrs Venetia Stanley." He claimed the Earl of Dorset, a title Sackville inherited after his brother's death, "kept [her] as his concubine, had children by her, and settled on her an annuity of £500 per annum; which after Sir K. D. married was unpaid by the earl; and for which annuity Sir Kenelm sued the earl, after marriage, and recovered it."

She undoubtedly did marry Sir Kenelm Digby, a man who had inherited his father's estate when his father had been executed for being part of the gunpowder plot! Sir Kenelm was a member of the Privy Council of Charles I, a privateer, and a scientist. We can thank him today for inventing a process to strengthen wine bottles. Venetia would take ill in 1633 and die from smallpox, but as she was dying Sir Kenelm had her painted on her deathbed by the famous artist Van Dyck, so he could remember her beauty long after she had departed this earth. Lord Sackville was to lead troops in the Thirty Years War in Europe for Frederick, King of Bohemia – whose Scottish wife Elizabeth Stuart was the daughter of King James VI and I – and in the English Civil War, get involved in the colonisation of North America, and was to die in London in 1652 at the age of 61 years.

How much truth there is in the story that the duel was fought over Venetia Stanley, I do not know. Try as I might, I could find no reference to what Sir Edward Sackville's wife thought of the whole matter, and I'm sure when he returned from Holland he wished he had been killed himself.

But this tale doesn't end here, King James VI and I, saddened by the loss of Edward Bruce and the waste of his life in the duel, asked his attorney general Francis Bacon to take up measures to outlaw the act of duelling. Using the pretext of a duel between two non-aristocrats, it was taken up in the Star Chamber 26th January 1615, and Bacon used the case to fire a warning at the aristocracy.

He told the Star Chamber:

> My Lords, I thought it fit for my place, and for these times to bring to hearing before your Lordships some cause touching private duels, to see if this Court can do any good to tame and reclaim that evil which seems unbridled. And I could have wished that I had met with some greater persons, as a subiect for your censure. But finding this cause on foot in my predecessor's time, and published and ready for hearing, I thought to lose no time, in a mischief that groweth every day; and besides it passeth not amiss sometimes in government, that the greater sort be admonished by an example made in the meaner, and the dog to be beaten before the lion. Nay I should think (my Lords) that men of birth and quality will leave the practice, when it begins to be vilified and come so low as to barbers-surgeons and butchers, and such base mechanical persons....

Bacon's points of attention were...

1. The nature and the greatness of this mischief
2. The cause and remedies.
3. The justice of the law of England, which some stick not to think defective in this matter.
4. The capacity of this court where certainly the remedy for this mischief is best to be found.
5. Mine own purpose and resolution...

Holding forth on the first point, Bacon argued: "When revenge is once extorted out of the Magistrate's hand contrary to God's ordinance…and every man shall bear the sword not to defend but to assail, and private men begin once to presume to give law to themselves, and to right their own wrongs, no man can foresee the dangers and inconveniences that may arise and multiply thereupon. It may cause sudden storms in Court, to the disturbance of his Majesty, and unsafety of his person."

On the second point, he said: "Touching the causes of it; the first motive no doubt is a false and erroneous imagination of honour and credit; and therefore the King, in his last proclamation, doth most aptly and excellently call them, bewitching duels. For, if one judge of it truly, it is no better then a sorcery that enchanteth the spirits of young men, that bear great minds, with a false show, *species falsa*; and a kind of satanical illusion and apparition of honour; against religion, against law, against moral virtue, and against the precedents and examples of the best times, and valiantest Nations."

Turning to the most effective ways of suppressing the evil of duelling, Bacon made a number of suggestions: "The first is, that there do appear and be declared a constant and settled resolution in the State to abolish it. For this is a thing (my Lords) must go down at once, or not at all: For then every particular man will think himself acquitted in his reputation, when he sees that the state takes it to heart, as an insult against the King's power and authority, and thereupon hath absolutely resolved to master it…in my conscience there is none that is but of a reasonable sober disposition, be he never so valiant, (except it be some furious person that is like a firework) but will be glad of it, when he shall see the law and rule of State disinterest him of a vain and unnecessary hazard."

The best remedy would be banishment from the Court: "This offence (my Lords) is grounded upon a false concept of honour, and therefore it would be punished in the same kind...The fountain of honour is the King, and his aspect, and the access to his person continueth honour in life, and to be banished from his presence is one of the greatest eclipses of honour that can be; if his Majesty shall be pleased that when this Court shall censure any of these offences in persons of eminent quality, to add this out of his own power and discipline, that these persons shall be banished and excluded from his Court for certain years, and the Courts of his Queen and Prince, I think there is no man that hath any good blood in him, will commit an act that shall cast him into that darkness, that he may not behold his Sovereign's face."

After much discussion and analysis, Bacon concludes:

Therefore now to come to that which concerneth my part, I say, that by the favour of the King and the Court, I will prosecute in this Court in the Cases following.

If any man shall appoint the field, though the fight be not acted or performed.

If any man shall send any Challenge in writing, or any message of Challenge.

If any man carry or deliver any writing or message of Challenge.

If any man shall accept or return a Challenge.

If any man shall accept to be a second in a Challenge, of either side.

If any man shall depart the Realm with intention and agreement to perform the fight beyond the seas.

If any man shall revive a quarrel by any scandalous bruits or writings contrary to a former Proclamation published by his Majesty in that behalf.

The Star Chamber accepted Bacon's arguments and announced that it was issuing a decree:

And finally, the Court showing a firm and settled resolution to proceed with all severity against these Duels gave warning to all young noblemen and gentlemen that they should not expect the like connivance or toleration as formerly have been, but that justice should have a full passage without protection or interruption...

And to that end the Justices of Assize are required by this honourable Court to cause this decree to be solemnly read and published in all the places and sittings of their several Circuits, and in the greatest assembly, to the end that all his Majesty's subjects may take knowledge and understand the opinion of this honourable Court in this case, and in what measure, his Majesty, and this honourable Court purposeth to punish such as shall fall into the like contempt and offences hereafter.

Alas it didn't do much to stop the duels, they still happened as before.

Further reading

State Trials James I Vol. II – 1603-27, pp. 1034-1045

Culross and Tulliallan its history and antiquities Vol I...David Beverage...1885. p150-156

Edward Sackville...letters 1613

[Beverage's book is on "Electric Scotland" — see e.g. Spartacus Educational for Venetia Stanley — the idea that Sackville had an affair with Venetia we owe to John Aubrey!]

Chapter 8

There's Something about Mr Paterson

In 1486 a book was written called the *Malleus Maleficarum*. The combined efforts of two German Dominican friars, Jakob Sprenger and Heinrich Krämer, it was a book that would bring much calamity to the world over the next two hundred years.

There were still practising pagan religions in Europe, but the superior order of Christianity couldn't have the competition of other lesser religions in its lands. The practisers of this religion were labelled witches and by blending phrases from the Bible, these two monks constructed a definition in their book to root out and destroy members of this false faith using methods from their manuscript. It was offered to Pope Innocent VIII, who agreed to the idea in principle. He wrote out a Papal Bull but refused to sign it. The witch-hunts were made legal through this Bull. The Pope's blessings granted it status as a legal document.

In Germany, the book was printed. One of the releases from John Gutenberg's new invention of the printing press, it was a must-have for parish priests, and armed with this doctrine the witch-hunts started in earnest.

To find someone guilty of witchcraft, the parishes needed confessions. In a nation of highly illiterate individuals, all it took was a signature to an already prepared written confession, or at least some mark they could put to register their name.

If even that was not forthcoming, a confession could be gained by the use of a fair degree of inventive torture. This is what the *Malleus Maleficarum* excelled in: a plethora of inventive methods to hurt and maim, and to gather the desired confession. Once the pain of torture had abated, a further signature without torture was needed. With the two signatures to the confession, the parish courts could now terminate the confessed witch with a public burning.

In the rules of the *Malleus Maleficarum* book, another method could be used to confirm the allegation of being a witch, and if the procedure was properly witnessed it could bypass the confessing signatures and still have the victim branded legally as a witch. It was regarded as absolute infallible proof. No regard was paid to protests of innocence from the bemused and hurt "witch". Proof was final and absolute!

The method of finding your witch, taken from the pages of the *Malleus Maleficarum*, was to find the witch's teat, or mark. The individual under suspicion of witchcraft could be thoroughly examined, and if a mark like a nipple, wart or mole was found after a physical search of the accused's body, a pin or bodkin would be inserted into the suspicious area by a special interrogator brought for purpose at great expense – the witchpricker!

In England the notorious Mathew Hopkins and his servant John Stern were in business in South West England during a short period between 1645–47 as professional witch prickers, dispatching over two hundred women and

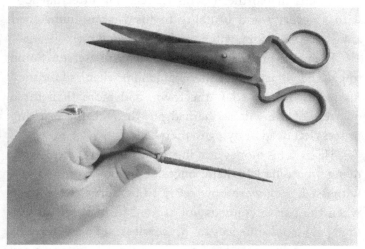

Witchpricker hair scissors and from 1704 Pitenweem witch trials.

several men to the gallows as witches. The period is captured in a diary John Stern wrote about doing "God's work".

In Scotland, John Kincaid from Tranent made a living out of it from 1633 to 1662. His known tally is (from my research) one hundred and ten witches killed and burnt. But his records are very incomplete, with I'm certain many hundreds more to be added to his tally that history has lost.

Many opportunists and freelance prickers were now following John Kincaid's lead and getting involved in the gory and lucrative business of witch finding in Scotland. Names such as John Bain begin to appear in the Parish court records, John Bain being noted as a great rival of Kincaid's, as well as a peculiar Highland gentleman doing the rounds in Northern Scotland, causing utter havoc – with a severity and brutality to his victims unmatched anywhere, even for a witch pricker and torturer!

His name in the record books was Mr Paterson. Some towns and villages, once this Highland pricker had finished his handiwork and left the town, had more than three quarters of the witches he had put through the pricking process left dead or dying in their cells.

He took his money, leaving the wasted wretches slowly dying where he left them; once the mark was found and witnessed, they were now ready to be burnt at the stake when the parish councils got around to it! Paterson was then paid handsome fees for his services, at £6 a witch plus expenses. At a time when a labourer earned a penny a day for hard toil in the fields, it was indeed quite a windfall.

Once paid, he wandered off to the next village or town where he would seek out more witches, ready to start his bloody work again. But there was something not quite right about this man and his two travelling servants.

Basically the whole direction of finding witches was instructed by the *Malleus Maleficarum* as being aimed at women. It is unbelievable in the extreme how this Highland pricker could wander at will with his two helpers through the towns causing such total carnage to the victims accused of witchcraft, while also being treated with respect and so lavishly wherever he went. Much hatred was directed, for example, towards accused witches blamed for infant mortality, famine, and shipwrecks. Maybe the brutality dished out to the victims was believed to demonstrate the pricker's superior knowledge of what he was doing, which was unquestionable to the baillies and councils. Did they see the suffering the witches got from the hands of the pricker as justice being served, with no questions to be asked?

Certain items mentioned in the witch finders' book the *Malleus Maleficarum* are so anti-women that its authors' mothers must have wondered what they had brought into the world! What could they have thought of them? The book quotes phrases from the Bible to sustain its jurisdiction on the persecution of women as witches: "There is no head above the head of a serpent; and there is no wrath above the wrath of a woman" (Ecclesiasticus xxv). The book comments: "I would rather dwell with a lion and a dragon than to keep house with a wicked woman" and concludes "all wickedness is but little to the wickedness of a woman."

Commenting on a text from Matthew xix, the book declares: "What else is woman but a foe to friendship, an inescapable punishment, a necessary evil, a natural temptation, a desirable calamity, a domestic danger, a delectable detriment, an evil of nature painted with fair colours".

The book quotes Seneca's *Tragedies* as saying: "a woman either loves or hates; there is no third grade. And the tears of a woman are a deception, for they may spring from true grief, or they may be a snare. When a woman thinks alone, she thinks evil."

The *Malleus* claims that all wickedness is but little to the wickedness of a women as they waver in their faith. Because women were made from Adam's rib in Eden, women are defective, the rib is bent therefore so are women, it shows the crookedness of women, and they are quicker to waver in their faith, they possess weak memories and vindicate themselves by the act of witchcraft.

The book rants on in this manner for many chapters, and it's this hatred of women that spurred on the witch hunts. Single old bewildered women made easy targets for accusing as witches, to be tortured for false confessions which would give up members of their supposed coven who would soon undergo the same gory procedure in the invisible conveyor-belt of death, ending around several stakes tied to tar barrels with a baying mob watching the women burn.

Certain fossils can be found around the coast of Britain on particular beaches. They were commonly known as the Devil's Toenails. By showing these, church ministers held congregations in awe at conclusive proof that the Devil was in the area. The Latin name is *Gryphaea arcuata* from the Sinemurian, Lower Jurassic age. In an age before there was knowledge about fossils, these did indeed look like some mighty beast's claws!

The Devil's Toenails, *Gryphaea arcuata* fossils.

Inverness is where in 1661 the dreaded Highland pricker Mr Paterson had arrived. He had travelled with his two servants around Highland towns and villages leaving a trail of death wherever he went. But a surprise of the most interesting and unbelievable kind was about to be revealed to the council members and baillies of Inverness, one that was unprecedented in the annals of witch finding. I quote directly from the source...

"There came then to Inverness one Mr Paterson, who had run over the kingdom for trial of witches, and was ordinary called the Pricker, because his way of trial was with a long brass pin. Stripping them naked, he alleged, that the spell spot was seen and discovered. After rubbing over the whole body with his palms he slipped in the pin, and, it seems, with shame and fear being dashed, they felt it not, but he left it in the flesh, deep to the head, and desired them to find and take it out. It is sure some witches were discovered, but many honest men and women were blotted and broken by this trick."

In Elgin, Paterson left two women Barbara Innes and Mary Collie dead in the cells after his pricking; in Forres another two women died, being Isobel Elder and Isabel Simson, and one witch called Margaret Duff who survived his treatment to burn later in Inverness.

He came to the parochial district of Wardlaw and found fourteen women and one man. Another four alleged witches were brought from nearby Ferintosh. They all had their heads shaved – all nineteen of them – amassing a "heap of hair" which was hidden in a stone dyke. After using his own unsavoury methods to gain a confession, he left the village leaving them in the prison more dead than alive after pricking them.

He found ten more witches, leaving eight further dead in the jails after he finished with them, before he moved on to pastures new with his expenses and vast profits pocketed with the job done. In the *Chronicle of the Frasers* it is stated that "this villain gained a great deal of mony having two servants".

For a man to go by the *Malleus* rules in searching women for the devil's marks, and with the extreme cruelty evidenced in this case, it is almost unbelievable that Mr Paterson with a few years under his belt of doing this profession was finally exposed as actually being a woman!

Being in a man's disguise, she brutalised her victims with a ferocity unprecedented even in the cruel years that those were. It seems to have been in Inverness that she was finally exposed.

I couldn't really make any sense of this case: the authorities were not too pleased to be part of this deception; but even with such a scandalous deception and so many being fooled by Paterson, no female name was given for her after being exposed, apart from Mr Paterson.

The base source of this information is the book *The Chronicle of the Frasers, the true genealogy of the Frasers,* which was written by James Fraser in 1674, not too long after the case.

The information has been shared by many. The first real documentation of witches was in 1830 with Sir Walter

Scott's book *Daemonology and Witchcraft*. George Black's excellent book *Calendar of Cases of Witchcraft* came later, in 1938. It follows the same details, and since then authors have mentioned the curious tale of Mr Paterson in many books. A BBC Radio Scotland programme repeated the Paterson story in 2012. Every other follow-up has followed the same procedure, taking the *Chronicle of the Frasers* as the source of information. No one has questioned the details of "Mr Paterson" being found out. Until now!

What we have to acknowledge about her is that her deception and the fact that she managed to continue it for so long without being detected, suggest an amazing piece of brilliance by her or absolute foolishness on the part of the parishes that sponsored her. In history, women with this type of ferociousness and lust for blood are very rare indeed. Of course, one can look at the case of the Hungarian Countess Bathory, who bathed in the blood of virgins, killing over six hundred of her servants, or that of Amelia Dyer in England in 1879 who murdered over sixty infants by strangling them and dropping them into local canals, while keeping the adoption money for them. But these are very rare examples. What turned Miss Paterson to the bloody business of witch pricking? And why use such merciless brutality on her victims?

Very little is known about this woman. With more background, we could have added to Scotland's gory past another character as infamous as Burke and Hare, the bodysnatchers of Edinburgh.

But she and her servants must have had a bitter ending. I went through witch trials and parochial records around the parishes of Inverness to find any information on the Mr Paterson case. But all I found in relevance to the name Paterson was an Agnes Paterson in Fisher Row in Lothian who burnt with two others around the same time as witches.

If "Mr Paterson" was taken to be judged in the capital, could this have been him, or her? Mr Paterson was responsible for the deaths of at least 36 people we know about, but how many others died in this deception is unknown. Things just did not seen right in the Mr Paterson case, so I took my research further to the National Archives of Scotland and got in contact with Louise Yeoman, a writer, curator and generally very helpful person, in charge of the manuscripts at the National Library.

With a request for information on the Paterson case offered to Louise, I got more than I ever hoped, and now, thanks to Louise's hard work searching for me, I can smash the myth of Mr Paterson for good! The key to Mr Paterson is that there was no such person as Mr Paterson! There was a man apprehended in Inverness as a witch pricker, and indeed found out to be a woman in disguise. But this woman was travelling under the name of John Dickson (or Dick). The name Paterson, it seems, is a rogue reference added to the book the *Chronicles of the Frasers* thirty years after the book was finished in 1674 and when the original author was dead. Some unknown editor rashly named the pricker in Inverness as being a Mr Paterson.

Primary sources written in the year 1662 know of only John Dickson or Dick working in Inverness under licence for finding and pricking witches. One source tells us that John Hay, an old man from the Parish of Dornoch of 60 years of age and untarnished reputation, fell into the hands of John Dick, having been accused of sorcery by a woman whose words were not worth heeding. John Dick shaved him, pricked him and tortured him. Then he sent him two hundred miles to the Tolbooth in Edinburgh, to be jailed pending further proceedings. The case against him was not considered strong enough by magistrates, and he was released despite John Dick's protests. He was under no illusion that the magistrates were very unhappy at his persistence and at the brutality unnecessarily handed out to Mr John Hay.

John Dick's career was folding fast. A warrant was issued for the arrest of John Dickson by the magistrates at Inverness and to transfer him to Edinburgh on the 19th May 1662. The council soon unmasked John Dick as a woman in disguise, and she was named as Christian Caddell who was masking as "John Dickson Burgess of Forfar". She is on record as being prosecuted for oppressing the king's subjects by counterfeiting her sex and giving out herself to have skill to know and try witches.

Her confession, with the contract to prick witches, in the name of John Dickson is in manuscript at the National Archives of Scotland.

The Register of the Privy Council knows her as "John Dick", under which male alias a complaint is logged against her activities. A copy of Christian Caddell's own confession is there too, with her calling herself "John Dickson Burgess of Forfar".

No reference whatsoever exists to the name of Mr Paterson: it is only the mistake in the book *Chronicles of the Frasers* that gives the Paterson name, to which so many references have been made by writers, who have not thought to dig a bit deeper to get the facts right.

Thanks to Louise at the National Archives of Scotland and me being a tad inquisitive, we have solved the Paterson mystery.

The Paterson reference is most certainly a faulty reference added years after the event, and confusingly added to great effect to forthcoming writings. Christian Caddell's confession was taken in the great Tolbooth of Edinburgh while she was in jail. It now sits in the National Archives of Scotland with her confirmation of imprisonment.

For such heinous crimes I'm surprised she wasn't accused of using witchcraft herself in forming her guise and bewitching those parishes where her male shadow walked and did her gory business. Christian Cadell alias John Dickson was allowed to survive. As documents from Edinburgh reveal, she was eventually transported to the colony of Barbados.

The records show that Christian Caddell, a prisoner from Edinburgh Correction House, was transported by Morris Trent, a merchant in Leith, from Leith to Barbados, on the *Mary* of Leith, master David Couston, on 4 May 1663.

In records, Caddell says she witnessed John Kincaid pricking in Newburgh in Fife in 1661. By comparison with her victims, Christian Caddell got off very lightly. On the very day her ship left Leith harbour, back in Forres two of her surviving victims Isobel Elder and Isabel Simson were both burnt to death. Although Christian had been arrested on charges of "giving out herself to have skill in the trying of witches", all those she had tortured to confess as witches still had their sentences carried out. In the records they died protesting their innocence to the bitter end. We find a written entry in the diary of Alexander Brodie of Broadie he states "they died obstinate".

Christian Cadell's story stops at Barbados. But someone somewhere should check the Barbados records and it would be interesting to find out what befell this nightmare of a woman. Did she even survive the voyage?

The man whose dreadful treatment by Christian Caddell alerted the Edinburgh magistrates and brought down "John Dick", ending the deceitful witchpricker's career, was John Hay from Dornoch. He never saw justice carried out on his abuser as he died from an infection from his pricking wounds and the brutality she put on him.

The Inverness old tolbooth was reconstructed in 1791 by Provost William Ingles of Kingsmills. The original tolbooth jail stood here from 600 AD. Beneath the ground are four small cells with standing space just four feet long. They had a slit to the pavement where food could be thrown down to them. Christian Caddell's victims were kept here.

There had been many commissions granted by Parliament to witch prickers working in parishes. But fees of £6 per witch motivated many a greedy fellow with no intention but murder and money in his mind. John Balfour was one such: he gained infamy when he was caught out for fraud as a witch pricker in 1632. He used spring-loaded pins that disappeared inside the mechanism meaning that no blood would come from the victim and she wouldn't cry out in pain. These would be taken as serious evidence of witchcraft.

Balfour joined the Newcastle pricker Cuthbert Nicolson as a "wicked fraudster". Nicolson was chased from Newcastle and later caught and hanged. They examined thirty accused witches and found exactly thirty witches...that meant a mind-numbing £180 for two weeks' work. That was a lot of money in those days, if you bear in mind that a teacher at that time earned £10 a year!

Christian Cadell alias John Dickson (later misnamed Mr Paterson) would join this shameful list of brutal fraudsters who were trading in death. At last the councils and communities began to see reason, and more fraudsters were exposed and joined the shameful list, such as James Welsh who was publicly whipped through the streets of Edinburgh in 1660 for falsely accusing a woman of witchcraft.

Returning to John Kincaid, I will now give a brief history on his movements as he pops up in the records of small towns and villages seeking out witches.

In Haddington May 9th 1661, "Nicall and Issobell Richardsone, Elspeth Lawsone and Issobell Cairne are dilated as guilty and apprehendit for the abominable sin of witchcraft." From there his career blossomed into a very lucrative business indeed.

In August 1661, John Kincaid is mentioned in the

parish of Newbattle where he found Isobel Fergusson guilty of witchcraft.

Other records state seven more women in August 1661 being burnt for witches in Haddington and John Kincaid being the pricker, but little remains of the trial records.

In the parish of Dalkeith from June–September 10th 1661, John Kincaid is in action again.

Confession of Jonet Watsone, Christine Wilsone and Janet Pairson, all accused of witchcraft. Despositions of John Kincaid in Tranent "the common pricker" as to finding the Devil's mark on Janet Peirson who was accused by Grissel Scott, a confessing witch.

It didn't take long before Kincaid had added Elspeth Graham, Janet Cock, Christian Wilson, and then Janet Clark to the cells of Dalkeith. In August he added Janet Millar, Janet Kerr, Helen Cass, Isobel Ramsey, Margaret Huchison, Jean Dixon, and Jonet Millar to the now crowded cells of Dalkeith. All were tortured by Kincaid in what seems to have been a big payday for him. All were burnt. Some details exist about allegations against Janet Cock...

Janet Cock was said to have an ill name, she bewitched William Scott's horse worth pounds and pounds of money and made him mad. She told a brute who beat her "he should live to be hanged" and this not very unlikely prediction was fulfilled. She kept company with the Devil on terms no honest woman should endure. She and Jean Dixon, another witch, cured a child by cutting off a dog's head, with which they made some Devilish spell that healed the bairn.

Dalkeith parochial records explain...

John Kincaid the public pricker was sent for to examine this person. He was deeply sworn on his solemn oath, went about his duties, and swore that he would do nothing in that connection but what was true. He found two marks on her, one on her throat, and one on her left arm. He pricked them without any feeling or sensation on her part, or the least appearance of blood. The holes stayed open and unclosed, as if the pins had been put in white paper.

Janet Cock was judged too dangerous to be at large and was put in prison to await trial. Strangely she was acquitted of all charges brought against her in court, but on the order of Kincaid she was not released but was kept in jail till a fresh charge could be brought against her. She sat chained and wasting in the jail cells.

A further charge did come against her on September 10th 1661. The deposition read...

There being an outcast [quarrel] betwixt you and Jean Forrest, because she had called you a witch, you came to the said Jean, her landlord's house, where she was with some neighbours, desiring to make "aggriement" between you. You maliciously and bitterly girning and gnashing your teeth and beating your hands upon your knees, said, "Oh them that called me a witch! Oh them that called me a witch!" And at that time, the said Jean Forrest, her child being in good health, on the morn the child, by your sorceries and witchcraft died; and the mother, at the child's departure, called out with a loud voice upon her neighbours, saying, "Alas! that ever I had ado with that witch Janet Cock, for she has been at my bedside all the night standing, and I could not get rid of her: and behold the fruit of it – my child is dead.

The charge was made and she was burnt with the others. It would be on John Kincaid's suggestion, the pricker being the one that got the confessions, and on his evidence that Janet Cock remained in jail till further accusations. The woman, once in Kincaid's hands, stood no chance of gaining her freedom!

In Aberdour, in September, from the Kirk sessions it states three witches are apprehended and the Reverend Robert Bruce calls for "the brodder" (Scots for "the witch pricker") and the witch pricker is sent for. Margaret Cant, Margaret Currie, and Janet Bell were worked on by the pricker and sentenced to burn to death as witches. The Earl of Morton tried to save them; he asked if "they should be set at liberty". He was overruled by the church, as the pricker claimed to have found the Devil's mark on all three.

No name is given to the active pricker engaged in the trial, but if they used Kincaid before in 1650 we can perhaps assume he was called back to this parish to continue his work.

In September 6th 1661 from the parish of Ormiston only two out of eleven witches that had been worked on by Kincaid ten months ago, were left alive in the cells of the town jail in Musselburgh.

Out of Marion Grinlaw, Elspeth Halliburton, Jean Hunter, Jean Getgood, Jean Knox, Margaret Hawie, Bessie Turnbull, Katherine Johnstone, John Harlaw, William Hog, and Jean Howison, only Marion Grinlaw and Jean Howison were left alive. The others perished with the wounds received during Kincaid's actions and with cold and starvation.

It is recorded that the survivors of ten women and one man who had been imprisoned at Musselburgh petitioned the Privy Council for their release. Most had died of cold and hunger and had lain in endurance of forty weeks, hence were in a state of extreme misery although nothing could be brought against them.

This was probably a case of Kincaid finding his mark on the "witches", being paid and moving on leaving the authorities to finish off the "witches" on their own initiative. But in this case we see the parish authorities did not have enough evidence, or perhaps more evidence was pending with the witches left in jail till the court could proceed again. Or maybe, just maybe, they were suspicious of Kincaid's verdict on the eleven accused!

In November 1661, Kincaid was seen in Newburgh by Christian Caddell applying his trade to two women, Margaret Liddle and Katherine Key, who confessed after he worked on them. The outcome is not noted but most likely they were burnt. It was here that Christian Caddell met and admired John Kincaid's work. Her fascination with his work would lead her to move to Inverness and disguise herself as Mr John Dickson, gaining a licence as a witch pricker and causing her own mayhem up there. For five more years Kincaid would carry on terrorising villages up and down the highways of Scotland. He would receive the keys to the town of Forfar for his sterling work, a fine honour, but he left.

I recently visited the Inverness Tolbooth jail where Christian Caddell alias John Dickson tortured and killed many of her victims. The Tolbooth today is a small tourist centre, but two small rooms still exist downstairs, split with two other rooms that were the jail cells, that are now part of the building next door. The rooms are not open to the public, but I thank the proprietor for allowing me access.

Further reading

Malleus Maleficarum...J Sprenger and H Krämer, 1489

Mr Paterson...Chronicle of the Frasers, ward law manuscript.

Christian Caddell—shipped to Barbados as prisoner, BARBADOS AND SCOTLAND links 1627-1877, p. 16

Christian Caddells...Archives of Scotland...Louise Yeoman

Mr Paterson...Calendar of cases of Witchcraft in Scotland 1510-1727

G. Black Haddington...Witches...Calendar of cases of Scottish Witchcraft in Scotland

G. Black Haddington...Witches...Devils Ain, Roy J.M.Pugh

Devils toenails... Gryphaeidae, Gryphaea arcuata... author's collection

Janet Cock...Witch stories...E Lynn Linton...1861

Aberdour Witches...Bygone Fife...James Wilkie, 1931

Aberdour Kirk sessions 1650-1661

Newburgh Witches...register of Privy council

Amelia Dyer...The woman who murdered babies for money...Alison Rattle /Allison Vale

Chapter 9

The Brahan Seer

Nothing beats getting away for a week, heading to the Highlands of Scotland to a rented cottage in a one-street village. Using the house as a base, my partner and the dog head out in the car with a detailed plan of nothing in mind, bar "head east today": while I navigate with a map, my partner drives. Nothing in front of us but adventure! Old churches, battlefields, remains of Pictish occupation and the many pottery places take our interest. We have brilliant walks in ancient Scots pine forests to keep the dog happy, and watch him leap about the heather in a lunatic frenzy.

Wild deer and pheasants, fog-shrouded mountains, and the mystique of the many standing stones, remnants of ancient Celtic Gods with scraped-in engravings, that have withstood thousands of years while the bones of their creators have turned to dust.

This is escapism at its best! Throw aside your phone and iPad for the week and ignore them; enjoy the freshest of food served in ancient castle restaurants, and then retire home to a log fire and a few beers. In 2015 our retreat up north took us to Marybank, a sweet street of a village with a warm pub called Balloan House which served breakfasts I am still yearning for a year later. My partner had an engagement in Fort William with an old friend, and I was on my own with my kids from London (long train journey) and we had no option but to explore Marybank on foot.

The Ordnance Survey map showed a ruined castle not

two miles from our house, so that's where our venture through forest and fern took us. Then it appeared: a stunning piece of architecture, a turret-laden fortalice straight from a movie scene…it was the ruins of the great Fairburn Tower.

A tall commanding structure, with four or five floors, looms before the visitor. Inside the staircase has perished, as has the roof. Fireplaces positioned on each floor can still be viewed from inside looking up. The building has to be appreciated, but if you want to visit make it soon…a huge crack from subsidence has formed from top to bottom, going through the front entrance lintel. This grand structure will not last long in this condition, and its collapse will be spectacular: the way the damage has spread, the whole lot will give way and fall to complete ruin.

This was the home of the last great Seaforth family, a branch of the powerful Mackenzie clan. It was a family with a curse upon them contained in predictions of the future. A 'seer' who had been condemned to death in the 1660s made his prediction of the doom of the family, which involved a peculiar incident at this very castle.

The basis and main source of this story comes from a book written in 1871 by Alexander Cameron, *The History and Traditions of the Isle of Skye*. Alexander was a solicitor and the Procurator Fiscal at Lochmaddy. He gathered his sources from other authors and storytellers who for generations had carried on the old fireside tradition of tales and folklore during the dark nights of Scottish winters. This story was put together and written down by Cameron for the first time in its history, taken from a world where it had remained in myth and well-worn fireside stories for the previous two centuries. I bring you the story of the Brahan Seer, using Alexander's information, and only adding my photographs to freshen the story.

Our seer is regarded as having second sight, that is, the ability of seeing the future in certain aspects. Predicting was his gift, a gift that would bring about his own death, caused by a client of great power and wealth who basically disliked what he predicted about her husband, who was away on business in France.

Coinneach Odhar Fiosaiche is his Gaelic name, born on the Isle of Lewis, in the Parish of Uig and Land of Lews around the early years of the seventeenth century.

The story goes that his mother, while tending her cattle near the burial ground of Baile-na-Cille in Uig, came upon the ghost of a woman who could not return to her grave because a wooden staff had fallen across it. The apparition asked her to remove the walking staff, as she needed to go back to the earth. This request she complied with, but not before the ghost had given her the gift of a small, round, white stone with a hole in its middle. According to her, the ghost said, "Give this to your son and he will have the gift of divination."

It was from the point that she gave this stone to her son Coinneach that he claimed to have got the powers that were to bring him fame and bring him troubles. "Coinneach" is the Gaelic pronunciation of "Kenneth": I will keep him as Kenneth through the rest of the story because he is widely known today as Kenneth Odhar.

Having been born on the estates of the Seaforth family on Lewis, when he grew up he worked as a general labourer in the fields of the estate farms. It is said that he was shrewd and clear-headed, with an intelligence beyond his lowly position.

The first discovery of his gift created a tragic event. His landlord's wife was in the habit of belittling her staff, who were well off and affluent compared to her grubby land labourers. She was a constant stream of abuse and teasing, but Kenneth was more than a match for her wit, reducing her to being laughed at by her own lowly employees. This insult she could not take in her position. She decided she must make moves to rid herself of him...to poison him!

He was sent away to cut peat in the fields, the most common fuel in those treeless islands off the west coast. In his isolation, his dinner was sent out to him as he laboured, by the farmer's wife! He suddenly felt his white stone go cold in his pocket. When he took it out of his pocket and looked through the hole in the stone, to his amazement it revealed the treacherous intent of the farmer's wife.

Disturbed by the stone's vision, and now suspicious of his pie, he fed his dinner to his dog. It promptly wolfed the food down and then keeled over and died.

This was how, he said, he discovered his gift. In order to move out of reach of the farmer's wife, he crossed to the mainland and worked on a farm at Strathpeffer. The years went by and his fame grew, with night-time storytellers adding to his legend around the late-night fires.

It was in the 1660s after the restoration of Charles II,

Kenneth the 3rd Earl of Seaforth was in France, leaving his wife to run the lands around Dingwall and Brahan Castle. What was troubling the countess was the prolonged absence of her lord and husband. It had been too long since a letter had arrived from him, and boats from France had brought nothing but empty news. Her anxiety grew daily; months were turning into years.

It was against this background that one of her servants mentioned Kenneth Odhar and his unusual talent for predicting the future. An urgent message was sent to Strathpeffer summoning Kenneth immediately. If he could, he was to give the countess some tidings of the absent Lord and what was delaying his departure from Paris.

He presented himself to the countess at Brahan Castle. He was fed and offered fine wine, and every courtesy and comfort were given to him as a guest of the house. On learning of her wish to know about her husband in France, Kenneth Odhar put his white stone to his eye and looked.

"Fear not, Countess, your Lord is safe and sound, well and hearty, merry and happy."

She asked him to describe his appearance, to which Kenneth Odhar responded, "Be satisfied, ask no questions, let it suffice you to know your Lord is well and merry."

But this was not enough, because the countess could see Kenneth Odhar was hiding something. She demanded to know further information.

"He is in a magnificent room, in very fine company, and far too agreeably happy and employed at present to think of leaving Paris."

The countess pressed for further details, eager to

know more, and gradually becoming frantic with rage, guessing that the seer was holding information back from her.

He finally gave way. "As you will know that which will make you unhappy, I must tell ye the truth. My lord seems to have had little thought of you or of his children or of his Highland home. I saw him in a gay-gilded room, grandly decked out in velvets, with silks and cloth of gold, and on his knees before a fair lady, his arm round her waist, and her hand pressed to his lips."

At this revelation, there was a moment's silence from the countess! Then all the suspicions and grief came together as one, and from the countess came nothing but anger and hatred. She was a woman scorned and her wrath was now mighty, but with no husband to direct it at, there in front of her was the figure of Kenneth Odhar who had just opened the wound in the countess's heart!

This moment had been witnessed by others, clan members and household servants. Lady Seaforth's humiliation was absolute, her despair was laid bare for all to see. Full of rage, she now directed her anger, and it was towards poor Kenneth Odhar, who stood astonished at her furious response. For her words spoken to Kenneth Odhar at this moment, I will take them straight from Alexander Cameron's book...

"You have spoken evil of dignities, you have defamed a mighty chief in the midst of his vassals; you have abused my hospitality and outraged my feelings, you have sullied the good name of my lord in the halls of his ancestors, and you shall suffer the most signal vengeance I can inflict – you shall suffer the death!"

A much astonished Kenneth Odhar, expecting at the very least a fee for his visions, was instead rudely led in chains to the castle dungeons. It was here that he looked into his white stone again and saw visions of the future, a future that did not read well for the Seaforth family...

I see into the far future, and I read the doom of the race of my oppressor. The long-descended line of Seaforth will, ere many generations have passed, end in extinction and sorrow. I see a chief, the last of his house, both deaf and dumb. He will be the father of four fair sons, all of whom he will follow to the tomb. He will live careworn and die mourning, knowing that the honours of his line are to be extinguished forever, and that no future chief of the Mackenzies shall bear rule at Brahan or in Kintail. After lamenting over the last and most promising of his sons, he himself shall sink into the grave, and the remant of his possessions shall be inherited by a white-coifed (or whitehooded) lassie from the east, and she is to kill her sister. And as a sign by which it may be known that these things are coming to pass, there shall be four great lairds in the days of the last deaf and dumb Seaforth – Gairloch, Chisholm, Grant and Raasay – one of whom shall be buck-toothed, another hare-lipped, another half-witted and the fourth a stammerer. Chiefs distinguished by these personal marks shall be the allies and neighbours of the last Seaforth; and when he looks around him and sees them, he may know that his sons are doomed to death, that his broad lands shall pass away to the stranger, and that his race shall come to an end.

After making this prediction, Kenneth Odhar on his way to his own execution threw his stone into a loch, saying that whoever found it would have similar gifts of visions.

It is known in the records of the Seaforth line from this date, there were actually four highland chiefs that supported the Earl of Seaforth when he arrived back on Scottish shores.

Sir Hector Mackenzie of Baronet of Gairloch was a well-known buck-toothed laird! The lords Chisholm of Chisholm, Grant, Baronet of Grant and Macleod of Raasay were all known for the other disabilities. The Seaforth Mackenzies are known to be descended from Irish stock, from an Irishman who was at the Battle of Largs in 1263 and who fought gallantly to help win the day against the king of Norway's men. He was awarded lands by Alexander III of Scotland in Kintail for his good service. The clan prospered at first, and then suffered the disasters of Flodden in 1514 and Pinkie in 1547.

Lord Seaforth fought for Charles II and was jailed for a while until his restoration in 1660. It was this chief and his overstaying exploits in France, that Kenneth Odhar claimed to have observed through his stone, thus angering his wife Isabella Mackenzie.

But the prophecies credited to Kenneth Odhar were

obscure in the years in which he made them, and some people must have made talk about how ridiculous and how downright laughable they were. They would in fact put a sober face on those who remembered the legend of the Brahan seer's tales at firesides many years later!

One amazingly accurate prediction credited to him follows...

> The day will come when the Mackenzies will lose all their possessions in Lochalsh and it will fall into the hands of an Englishman, who shall be distinguished by great liberality to his people, and lavish expenditure of money. He will have one son and two daughters; and, after his death, the property will revert to the Mathesons, is original possessors, who will build a castle on Druim-aDubh, at Balmacarra.

An Englishman, Mr Lillingstone, came into possession. He was truly distinguished for kindness and liberality to his tenants, and he had a son and two daughters. When he died, the son sold the whole estate of Lochalsh in 1851 to the member of parliament for Ross and Cromarty, a Mr Alexander Matheson. A castle was built at Duncraig but as yet none built at Druim-a-Dubh.

From William Anderson's book *The Scottish Nation* (Vol 3) we get a little more on this MP. He bought quite a bit of land including Eilean Donan Castle, which was nothing but a ruin at the time. It was noted that, unlike his English predecessor Mr Lillingstone, he was not so kind to his tenants and evicted most of them. He died in 1886.

Other predictions seemed incredibly obscure. They must have brought ridicule to the seer, so outlandish must they have seemed at the time. This next one fits in that category.

On the south coast of the bay of Petty, between the estates of Culloden and Moray sat in 1660 a giant boulder, at least eight tonnes in weight. The Brahan Seer predicted "that the day will come when the Stone of Petty, large though it is, and high and dry upon the land as it appears to people this day, will suddenly be found as far advanced into the sea as it now lies away from it inland, and no one will see it removed, or be able to account for its sudden and marvellous transportation."

On the 20th February 1799, one hundred and thirty-nine years after the seer's death, it was mysteriously moved from its position on land and carried 260 yards into the sea. It is supposed some earthquake or action of ice on that stormy night was responsible, but at the time it was blamed on the work of Satan.

Another of his predictions given while on business for the Seaforths in the Culloden district near Inverness, he gave a foresight into an incident that would occur 85 years after his death...

> Oh! Drummossie, thy bleak moor shall, ere many generations have passed away, be stained with the best blood of the Highlands. Glad am I that I will not see the day, for it will be a fearful period; heads will be lopped off by the score, and no mercy will be shown or quarter given on either side.

The location of Drummossie Moor is today otherwise known as Culloden Moor, the site of the fateful ending of the Stuarts' ambitions for the throne of Britain, with the massacre of the clans that happened here. On the 16th April 1746, 1,600 ill-led men would be killed on this land, defeated by 300 government troops – marking the end of Charles Edward Stuart's bid for power.

There are far too many more predictions credited to Kenneth Odhar to be listed here, but I will simplify some of the famous ones. The seer predicted, "I would not like to live when a black bridleless horse shall pass through the Muir of Ord."

Was this a prediction of the railway line that went through here in the nineteenth century?

The seer predicted, "When the big-thumbed Sheriff Officer and the blind man of the twenty-four fingers shall be together in Barra, Macneil of Barra may be making ready for flitting". This prediction was discussed about fireplaces and taverns in Barra for generations. A blind man left the island of Benbecula on a tour to collect alms; he had six fingers on each hand and six toes on each foot, giving him "twenty-four fingers". On the boat from South Uist to Barra, he met the Sheriff Officer, who in fact was carrying an eviction summons for the laird of Barra...a Mr Macneil! So precise is this prediction, the "blind", a 24-fingered man, did indeed meet the Sheriff Officer who doled out Macneil's expulsion order.

I must finish with the most important prediction given by Kenneth Odhar the seer on his way to execution.

He forecast the Seaforth family's end, and this must

have seemed utterly laughable when he gave the prediction. So laughable that it was remembered and passed down generation after generation until, in 1851, it actually happened.

A newspaper in Inverness recorded the events and published the amazing piece the week it happened. The seer's words were regarding the Mackenzies of Fairburn Castle, near Marybank today. The prophesy from Kenneth Odhar follows…

> Strange as it may appear to all those who may hear me this day, yet what I am about to tell you is true and will come to pass at the appointed time. The child unborn today will witness it. The day will come when the Mackenzies of Fairburn Tower will lose their entire possessions and that branch of the clan shall disappear almost to a man from the face of this earth. Their castle will become uninhabited, desolate and forsaken, and a cow shall give birth to a calf in the uppermost chamber in Fairburn Tower.

Now in 1660, when this prediction came forth from Kenneth Odhar, Fairburn Castle was occupied by a wealthy chieftain called Roderick Mackenzie, a rich and respected lord. There were halls resounding in music and tapestries of fine decor, and a spiral staircase going up five floors. There were servants and pageboys for every want, fine hunting dogs, and weaponry as decoration around roaring log fires. Homage from surrounding tenants was delivered here. Against this background a cow giving birth in the highest of the five floors was treated as the biggest laugh going!

But the Mackenzies' fortunes turned, because they threw in their lot with the Stuart kings in the two failed rebellions of 1715 and 1745. This saw the castles and estates taken from them by the Hanoverian monarchy. Fairburn Tower went to ruin in the 19th century after being deserted by the Stirling family for the newly built Fairburn House. In 1851 the castle was open to the elements, and the surrounding lands open to free range cattle farming. One of the cows somehow wandered into the castle, and proceeded to climb the spiral stairs, all five floors, till it nestled in the top turret and lay down in peace and comfort to give birth to its own calf! The cow's bellows were heard by a farmworker and the cow was found in its remarkable position.

Many witnesses came to see the spectacle, and more to the point Kenneth Odhar the Brahan Seer was finally given the respect he never received when alive.

In 1660 the Brahan Seer, Kenneth Odhar or Coinneach Odhar Fiosaiche, was taken in a cart to the Ness of Chanonry. There a tar barrel was waiting, filled with freshly boiled-up molten black tar. Additionally, iron spikes had been hammered into the barrel to heighten the cruelty. Tied by his hands and feet, Kenneth Odhar was dumped head-first into the boiling pitch and secured in place by the spikes. They piled up combustibles around the shocking scene and watched Kenneth Odhar's pathetic remains burn and illuminate the beach.

It is said that on the day the Brahan Seer met his death,

Lord Seaforth returned from France, heard of the events occurring at Chanonry point and as fast as his horse could take him hastened to the burning place to stop the proceedings. But thick black smoke was visible on the horizon before he reached the hellish scene.

It is a most incredible story. There are many more predictions credited to the Brahan Seer, but that must be for the reader to investigate in more detail in other books. I visited the castle and found it a remarkable structure – it is a shame that no one has tried to preserve it, but it would cost millions. The spiral stairs, the ones that the cow ascended to its place in the turret, have fallen. With the frontal structure showing advanced signs of attrition, one needs to make haste to appreciate the building before the next storm takes it down.

At Chanonry point a stone monument is preserved down at the beach near where poor Kenneth Odhar, the Brahan Seer, met his end in such a repugnant and violent action. It is worth seeing, and the scenery from here is beautiful, masking an ugly event that still echoes through the years. My last thought on the Brahan Seer is this…

If the Brahan Seer actually had the gift of foresight, why didn't he look through his white stone when summoned by the Countess of Seaforth and see his own fate through the stone's hole?

Fairburn Tower in 2015, showing turret where cow gave birth (left), and crack in the wall (right).

Brahan Seer memorial at Chanonry Point.
The plaque reads:

THIS STONE COMMEMORATES
THE LEGEND OF COINNEACH ODHAR
BETTER KNOWN AS THE
BRAHAN SEER
MANY OF HIS PROPHECIES WERE
FULFILLED AND TRADITION HOLDS
THAT HIS UNTIMELY DEATH BY
BURNING IN TAR FOLLOWED HIS FINAL
PROPHECY OF THE DOOM OF THE
HOUSE OF SEAFORTH

Chapter 10

Not on the Sabbath!

In old times, the sabbath was a day when strict rules were enforced that the population of towns and villages would attend church services – or else suffer the penalties for committing such a crime.

Church service could start at 9am, followed by another at 11am, then the afternoon 2.30pm service followed by the 5pm service...not forgetting the evening service. Looking back, the day of supposed rest now seems fraught with religious turmoil.

The church possessed the power to punish delinquents for a number of what we would regard today as completely laughable offences. But the penalties were serious enough. They usually included cash fine punishments, with every penny going into church coffers. It is no exaggeration to say that if the funds started to get thin, more persecution of sabbath breakers was the easiest way to nurse the coffers to better health.

In Inverness on the 10th of May 1697, such a condition of poverty in the church funds meant that the Session ordered:

> that there should be an intimation made from pulpit the next Lord's day, that if there be any found to extravage [wander] through the streets in time of Divine Service, whether children, that the parents of such children or masters of such servants shall

be comptable [accountable] for them and censured accordingly, as also to request the constables [be] careful and diligent to discharge the trust put into their hands.

More examples are to be found in the Kirk Session records.

Similarly, on 8th June 1701, the Session,

having considered the many grievances made by the Elders anent several who do extravage [wander] on the Sabbath day, particularly servants and children, did recommend to the Moderator that he intimate to masters of families that they restrict their children and servants, or otherwise they be proceeded against as breakers of the Sabbath.

And on 3rd June 1707, following complaints about Sabbath breaking, the Session:

appoint that these Elders who collect at the Church door on the Lord's day shall go about the Church and through the streets in time of public worship, forenoon and afternoon, to observe and delate [denounce] such as are guilty of profaning that day, and also that they go through the streets betwixt five and six afternoon from the beginning of March to the end of September, and do what in them lies for preventing of disorders upon the Lord's day.

On 8th April 1695:

the Session of the said burgh, being informed of several who in time of Divine Service went to the tavern houses, and there drank to excess, did pass act that whoever of the retailers of ale or any other strong liquors shall be found to retail either of the foresaid liquors in time of Divine Service, that they shall be liable to Kirk censure, besides other punishment that may be inflicted on them by the civil magistrate. As also it is hereby intimated to the uplifters of the Collections each Sabbath day, that four of them, viz., two in the forenoon and two in the afternoon, with two of the burgh officers, go through the town and tavern houses, and if they find any either extravaging or drinking on the Sabbath in time of Divine Service that they be delivered to the said officers and committed by them to prison till they be brought to Session or condign punishment.

Inverness had the Tolbooth Jail as a place to secure its declared rogues and villains. But it also had another unique jail for those who needed confinement of a solitary nature. That was the destination for special criminals, a place so horrid it was only fit for crimes such as murder…or sabbath breaking! It was a cell specially built under the stone arches of the Inverness Bridge over the River Ness, which had been built in 1685 (it took three years) for the price of £1,300. The cell was a concave hollow dug into the foundations of the third archway (the bridge had seven arches). It was twelve feet across and a most gloomy retreat:

cold, damp, and undesirable. It had only a metal grating for a window that looked up southward towards the river.

It had a stone bench for comfort and a small hole in the floor for a toilet, that dropped into the flowing river. Entrance to it came from the bridge itself with the cell opened by a heavy wooden hatch from the road. Traffic would thunder across here leaving the resident of the jail sleep-deprived and tormented. If that wasn't bad enough, further humiliation was added by the patrons of the town who found sport in lowering food on strings in front of the cell's barred windows. The poor starved wretch inside would grab fruitlessly for the scraps of bread and meat dangled about to add to the occupant's considerable misery.

It happened on 6th May 1691 that whispers of witchcraft were once again spreading through the town of Inverness. In the night, an effigy of a child made from clay had been found "with the shapes of a living child". The parish court "ordained all the persons of the Bucht and Kinmylies to be summoned to the Session the next Session day to clear themselves by oath of this base and un-Christian work"...On the 16th of June the people who had been summoned appeared at the Session and were urged by the moderator not to conceal the maker of the clay effigy, "knowing any that had a hand in it to be void of the fear of God, and to this effect the following were sworn to tell the truth...Andrew McKilleain, Marie Fraser, Janet Fraser, William McAlister, Donald Gow, Margaretnine Warran, Donald MacGilebie, Alexander Fraser, Christian McLean, Joan Schieviz, Anna McKillican, Christian McRabbie,

Marie Mc Murdow, John McFarquhar, Alexander Glassach, Katherine McLean, Hendrie Davidson, Alexander Fraser and Christian Clerk."

All the above were interrogated by the parish appointed magistrates, but there was universal denial of any knowledge of the clay doll. It may have been made as an innocent toy for a small child or it may have been part of some illicit form of *"maleficarum"*. But after much interrogation, the minister declared he knew no other way to extract the truth "till God in his infinite power was pleased to find it out".

In May 1691 a weaver by the name of John Clerk was reproved by the moderator for his "debauched carriage". Clerk promised to behave himself, under pain of imprisonment in the vault of the bridge if anyone saw him "debauch himself by swearing or drinking" – the imprisonment was to last for eight days during which he would only be fed on barley bread and water. We do not know if he mended his ways or ended up in the cell.

There was a tradition that a prisoner was once left in the cell under the bridge. His sentence served, once the trapdoor was opened they could get no response from the villain inside...an officer was lowered into the cell, where to his horror he found the inmate had died some days ago and his body had been eaten away by rats! Nothing was left but skin and bone.

The original bridge collapsed under a flooding of the river in 1849, all seven arches were washed away, including the jail. A new bridge was started in 1850 upon the same site as the old one and exists today.

Chapter 11

The Monster of Queensberry

Durisdeer Parish lies in the South West of Scotland in Dumfriesshire. It boasts a quaint old church whose history goes back to 1394, when its minister is acknowledged to have held his first service. The church vestry holds several tombs belonging to the Douglas family under their title of Marquis of Queensberry (a title which was given to the family in 1682 by Charles II, William Douglas being the first to bear the title).

They had a mansion near here called Kinmount House and several castles – Sanquhar Castle, built in the 13th century and Drumlanrig, built in the 17th century. Durisdeer Parish was used as a resting place and crypt for the family dead.

The title of Marquis of Queensberry, after William Douglas died in 1695, was bestowed upon his son James Douglas, who was also named the second Duke of Queensberry. He was born in 1662 and died in 1711. His body is here in the parish, as is that of his wife. His death saw him pass the title to his second son Charles, who was born 1698 and died 1778. But Charles had not been the next in line for the title.

There is another tomb that lies among those in the family crypt with the name James Douglas, 1697–1715. It is a tomb of massive length and breadth compared to the other family members beside him. James should have been the heir to the Queensberry fortune and castles they owned. But he was ignored! The inheritance was passed on to his brother Charles and not him.

This was the stain in the family: a child who was born to wealth and titles but who, by some misfortune, was born to a monstrous nature as a gluttonous hulk. He was as grotesque in form as a beast, uncultured and damaged within. He grew to an immense size, held away from the embarrassment of others and kept in locked rooms. He was unchained to be exercised in dungeons away from prying eyes.

James Douglas, the second Marquis, was heavily involved in pushing through the bill for the union of the Scottish and English parliaments with Lord Anstruther in 1706 and 1707.

He had already in 1706 brought into existence a charter of "Novodamus", through which a feudal superior may re-bestow a former grant under a new set of conditions. In this case his intention was to stop the title of marquis going to his eldest son James, who was the next in line, to disinherit him and give the title to his younger brother Charles instead.

The act was brought forward and on the death of James, the 2nd Marquis, it would indeed fall to Charles to be 3rd Marquis.

When the Act of Union was finally accepted in 1707, James the 2nd Marquis with his wife and family were out in Edinburgh celebrating. In the process of pushing through the Union, Lord Anstruther had pocketed £300 sterling, and the Marquis's fee must have been equally impressive.

(A town clerk at this time would expect a yearly wage of £2.15s.)

They had gone out from the family house at 64 Canongate – Queensberry House – leaving a few servants and James Douglas locked up in one of the upper rooms. The residence was a substantial three-storey building with an attic. It had been built in 1670 by Margaret Douglas and sold to William in 1689. The substantial attic was where James Douglas was allowed to stay.

Down in the basement where the kitchen was located, a young lad was left to oversee the baking and other preparations, as the older kitchen staff were all out with the Earl to celebrate in the pubs of Edinburgh. The cook's apprentice was left roasting a joint of meat on a spit for the night's dinner. The delicious smells of the meat wafted through the corridors above, teasing all who smelt the delicious aroma. It was too much for the aberration that was James Douglas. He broke his restraints and forced his attic door. The smell of roasting juices made him fumble his way downstairs towards the house kitchens. But when James Douglas found the source of the lovely smells…between him and the roasting dish was the kitchen boy.

The echoes of the high-pitched screams of the lad went unheard, as the large mansion house was empty.

It was the servants not an hour later who discovered the horrific scene in the kitchen. The monster figure of James Douglas was seated in front of the fire still turning the spit and roasting meat. But the creature had already eaten the original half-cooked roast and had replaced it by breaking the kitchen boy's neck, ripping his clothes off and spearing his puny body upon the spit as you would a capon or a pig! James Douglas was found in the act of pulling strips of half-burnt meat from the boy's body and eating it!

The kitchen staff managed to beat the monster back to his room and lock him in until the Marquis was called. The decision was made to relocate James Douglas to secure surroundings, so as not to create further embarrassment. He is known to have died under restraint in Woodall, West Yorkshire, on 24th January 1715. He had outlived his father to see his title awarded to his younger brother.

Queensberry House is in central Edinburgh by the Canongate area, and was until 2012 used as part of the Scottish Parliament Allowance office. Now it is used as a parliamentary bar for current MSPs and their guests. The kitchen in the basement that was host to the horrific sights of 1707 still exists, but it is not now in use. However, the oven spit that ended the life of the kitchen boy is still there, as is the attic where the demented beast was held.

The Queensberry name is better known now in connection with the rules of boxing. The 9th Earl, in 1865, (another James Douglas) gave his name to support several fundamental rules and the wearing of gloves in the sport. They have remained the "Queensberry Rules" to this day.

Further reading

The Queensberry Mansion and James Douglas... *Traditions of Edinburgh* ...R.Chambers 1868...p. 354-356

The Castles of Scotland ...Martin Coventry, Queensberry House...p. 556

What exists today of the cooking fireplace in Holyrood
House...where the young cook was killed and roasted!

Chapter 12

Half-Hangit Maggie

Newspapers and court records is where we head in order to reveal the fascinating history of 'half-hangit Maggie'. It is 1724 and the Fife coast fishing fleet has come to drop its catch in the port of Leith. The many baskets of mackerel, cod and herring are bought straight from the ships by merchants. From here the fish is taken up to Edinburgh, Scotland's capital, where it is sold by fish hawkers in the open street markets.

Margaret Dickson was 22 years old, born in nearby Musselburgh. She was brought up with a strong religious background. At this time in Scotland there have been two failed Jacobite rebellions, in 1715 and 1719, and the fear of papists is shouted from the pulpits of Edinburgh. Maggie is married to a fisherman and has two children. Her husband has been working from Newcastle; the loneliness of his long absence at a time when she needs the comfort of a man wears on her weary existence. It seems his posting in Newcastle has become permanent and in trying to stay nearer to him, she finds work in an inn in the border town of Kelso. But her vulnerable position leaves her heart open for carnal needs, the proprietor's son William Bell takes full advantage and – in a day where the crime of fornication carries heavy penalties from the lawmen of the church – the affair bears fruit!…Margaret is pregnant again, but with the child of William Bell.

Now "fornication" in Scottish law used to carry the

death penalty! The Adultery Act of 1563 in Mary Queen of Scots Parliament states...

"For sa meikle as the abominable and filthy vice and crime of adulterie has been perniciously and wickedly used within this realm in times by gone...it is statute and ordained...that all notour and manifest committers of adulterie...shall be punished with all rigour unto the dead."

At least one person fell to this act...

John Guthrie was prosecuted for the crime of notorious adultery. He was accused of having married a wife in the shire of Forfar, and deserted her; of having afterwards come to Leith; of having laid aside the name of Laird, which he bore in Forfar, and assumed that of Guthrie, and there marrying another wife, with whom he cohabited for several years; and also, of committing adultery with another woman. These facts he acknowledged before the Kirk-session of Kirkliston, and did penance in sackcloth for his impurities. – Being thus detected and stigmatized by the church, the secular arm was next stretched forth against him. A warrant under the royal sign manual, dated at Whitehall, 26th of January 1617, was directed towards the Lord Justice General, and the other Justices. It set for, that the King's Advocate, by his Majesty's express command, was about to prosecute the prisoner for the crime of notorious adultery, and required the Justices instantly, on his conviction, to condemn him to death. The Court had the humanity not to enter this warrant upon record till about a month after the

> prisoner's conviction, when it sentenced him to be taken to the Cross of Edinburgh, and hanged on a gibbet till he be dead; and he appears to have been carried to immediate execution.

As long as she could, Margaret Dickson hid the pregnancy behind heavy petticoats and undergarments. She carried on working as normal, but the coming scandal and the charges that would be thrown at her by the church, and the humility and shaming that would come with them, hung heavily over her. In this distressed state she gave birth prematurely. The baby was dead in her arms. A sad, sad figure she was now, but she had to keep it secret.

She stole away from the inn in the night and headed towards the river Tweed, that flows through Kelso. On the banks of the Tweed she bade her farewells to the little one who never woke up to see his mother's eyes. She placed him gently in the waters and with a tear let him slip away...

But the current only took the body into the tangle of the riverbank reeds, where it was found. Maggie was soon caught out as the bairn's mother and was at once arrested and brought to the Tolbooth in Edinburgh to await judgement! In court they charged her under the Concealment of Pregnancy Act 1690.

The charges were serious, her crime amounting to murder. Maggie was charged with hiding the child to prevent being made a public embarrassment and spectacle in the eyes of the church.

When a surgeon examined the dead child, he wrote for evidence that in his opinion the child had breathed. Water was drawn into the lungs, and the child had been alive when dropped into the river.

Maggie admitted the crime of fornication, and also that she had hidden the pregnancy for fear of being made a public example. She said she had gone into labour earlier than expected, and her pains prevented her from getting any assistance. She in her confusion could not say what happened to the child. As it was a capital crime, she was sentenced to be hanged in a market place in Edinburgh on the 2nd of September 1724.

A large crowd – as is usual for a hanging – is what meets Maggie Dickson as she walks out to the scaffold. She is still penitent but at the same time denies her guilt. The hangman John Dagleish puts the rope around her neck, turns it slightly to the side so the neck will snap after the six-foot drop…he kicks the lever holding the trapdoor, she falls, the crowd cheers and hats are thrown into the air. The body is cut down and a waiting doctor takes a pulse, and announces the expiry of poor Maggie Dickson. A coffin is brought forward and Maggie is placed inside.

Maggie's father Duncan and her friends have the coffin on a cart and it is now taken on its last journey. A burial plot is waiting in Inveresk cemetery. But a good send-off was traditional in Scotland and to celebrate what a miserable life she had, a wake is undertaken, stopping at each pub along the way to raise a glass to Maggie Dickson. At one tavern where they stop, two passing carpenters looking at the workmanship of the coffin are taken aback by unearthly noises coming from inside!

Her father Duncan opens the casket…and there is his

daughter and she sits up...she's alive! People run for their lives in horror, glasses smash, and chaos ensues amongst these godly people! Her father takes her home where he nurses her back to full health. In the eyes of the law, Maggie has served her sentence, and so she is allowed to go about her business.

I am relieved to say the Maggie Dickson story did have a happy ending. She was reunited with her husband in Newcastle and they eventually ran an alehouse in Berwick-upon-Tweed. They prospered and had another child ten months after her hanging, called James. Maggie lived to 1753.

A pub still stands in Edinburgh, not far from the spot where Maggie was hanged, and it carries her name and a plaque telling her story.

Chapter 13

The Great Orkney Farty Witch

When I lived in London, at the peak of summer my need to be near water in the heat of the day brought me down with friends to Wapping at the side of the River Thames: quaint narrow streets I'm sure long ago were less than welcoming, with press gangs and dubious characters straight from a Charles Dickens novel in the area's murky past. But from these winding ancient streets comes the most delightful string of English pubs with the history of the area wrapped up in stories of stolen crown jewels, murder and pirates.

One such pub is "The Prospect of Whitby", where with the beer garden to the back you can watch the river transports go up and down the River Thames. To the right of the pub stands an old gibbet, with a hangman's noose attached. This was once known as Execution Dock, where many an unfortunate was dished out his sentence from the courts and executed right here.

Many a convicted pirate dangled from here, and many were Scotsmen, perhaps the most famous being Captain Kidd from Dundee. He was actually hanged twice, as his first hanging broke the rope!

But I want to relate the history of another Scottish pirate, not so well known, and born in the islands of Orkney. This is the story of John Smith alias Captain Gow and his association with a witch from Stromness, who in herself was a legend, but not in the way the reader would recognise as the usual traits of a witch – this one was far more unusual.

John Gow was born in Orkney in 1698, and spent the early years of his manhood in merchant ships and on some men-of-war. When he joined his latest ship, a galley called the *George*, a ship of 200 tonnes and 20 guns, his position was second mate and gunner. On the first of August 1724, the ship sailed to Santa Cruz in Barbary from where she was to collect cargo and sail up the Mediterranean to Marseille. The captain of the ship, Captain Ferneau, was cruel and generally mean. He worked his men too hard and fed them the smallest rations of the cheapest food, while enjoying, in the comforts of his own cabin, the most luxurious cuisine. It did not take long for the crew to complain, and before long John Gow impelled the hatred towards mutiny.

With Captain Ferneau getting whispers of this dissent, he threatened severe floggings to the mutineers. By this time Gow had persuaded six of the crew to plan a rebellion: James Williams (a Welshman), Daniel McCawley (an Irishman), William Melvin (Scottish), Peter Rawlinson and James Winter (both Swedish) and John Peterson (Danish). The plan was to murder the captain and all his officers and seize the ship!

On the 3rd November the *George*, laden with wax and other goods, left the harbour of Santa Cruz, and at ten o'clock that night when the officers were asleep and only the captain was on watch, they struck. James Winter went downstairs to the surgeon's quarters, looking for Thomas

Guy; Peterson went to the chief mate's cabin to seek Bonadventure Jelphs; Daniel McCawley to another officer called Schrivan. On deck Melvin and Rawlinson seized the captain. The poor officers below had their throats slit by the named assassins, and the captain was to be thrown overboard. Below decks all the gory action seemed to go as planned, but above the captain put up an enormous desperate struggle. His throat had been cut but not deep enough, and he now wrestled with his would-be murderers, until Gow came to him and felled him with a pistol shot. The horror continued as the three officers who had been assaulted below decks came up the stairs with throats cut but very much alive. They were also dispatched by pistol and thrown overboard.

The other crewmates were threatened with death if there was any opposition to the mutiny. The ship was promptly renamed the *Revenge*, and they set out for a life of piracy and a quest for business.

The first prize they took was on the 18th of November – the *Cape St Vincent*, a ship from Newfoundland owned by Thomas Wise. But the ship was a merchantman laden with nothing but fish! This was of no great value to them, not the treasure they thought to find! Having no use for the cargo, they cannibalized the ship for spares, taking anchor and ropes off her, and then sank the vessel.

Some days later they came across a defenceless Scottish ship from Glasgow, again laden with herrings and salmon, destined for the port of Genoa. The captain was a Mr John Somerville. Again fish had no value to the pirates, so once again the crew was taken into the hold and the ship was sunk, so as to give no intelligence of their crime.

Two weeks later they saw a sail as big as their own ship, to which they gave chase. The boat had French flags and seemed laden with the spoils they had been seeking so intently...but three days' chase brought them into a fog bank near Madeira and the victim was lost to them. In need of provisions, they headed into the port of Porto Santo, where a large Portuguese ship was sitting.

They introduced themselves as British merchantmen and John Gow dined aboard with the Portuguese as Captain Somerville. During the pleasantries he unmasked himself and his associates as pirates and took the captain hostage. What goods they asked for were brought to them and they released the prisoners they had from the two merchant ships they had sunk.

Now refreshed with provisions they resolved to attack shipping again along the coast of Spain. What they had attacked as pirates so far had produced little or no riches for them. Deep water boats were there for a reason...fishing...but perhaps ships nearer the coastline might yield better goods. There was more chance of meeting a warship, but they thought the gain outdid the risk.

It only took two days for another ship to be quickly taken. This was a New England ship called the *Bachelor*, but once more the pirates came up empty.

The pirates were by now almost at the point of mutiny with their unlucky "Captain Smith", but in the next few days they finally struck gold, with the taking of the *Lewis and Joseph*, a French ship.

It was full of plunder and fine wines. They took the ship as their own and transferred the twelve-man crew into their own ship, into the hold which was now an overcrowded makeshift prison.

The next target did not take long to find, a large Portuguese trader, but Gow refused to attack it as it looked to have superior guns. This caused the Welsh pirate Williams to declare "Captain Smith" a coward, and a fight between then ensued.

Williams wanted to kill the prisoners, have them thrown overboard to lessen the weight, and then attack the ship! Williams aimed a pistol at John Smith's head but the flint never sparked. Williams in turn was shot in the arm and belly but made his way towards the powder room intending to blow up the ship. He was caught just in time and was subdued and put in irons. Williams joined the other prisoners in the hold.

Two days later another potential prize appeared on the horizon, a Newfoundland-bound ship called the *Triumvirate*. Once seized it was found to have a modest cargo, which was taken, and the rebel Williams was put aboard the ship in chains. The *Triumvirate* was then released, with some of her crew joining the pirates. They had previously sunk their victims to avoid the authorities getting news of their activities, and in fact it was their mercy towards this ship which sealed the pirates' doom. The next port the *Triumvarate* put in to, all would be told to the authorities about the rogue pirates and their whereabouts.

The decision was made by Captain Smith to head home, back to the Orkney Islands to hide until things calmed down again. There he knew the land and he could at least pass in the harbours there for a visiting trader.

It was here that Captain Smith met a laird's daughter, Miss Gordon: a romance soon blossomed, and his time in Orkney became longer than he had intended. Before long some of his crew in the taverns of Stromness, much inebriated with drink, talked about their past, and the magistrates were awakened to the rogues amongst them! Some of the pirates of Smith's crew were alerted to the impending arrests and took to their boat to escape to the ship, but before reaching it a custom-house boat full of soldiers caught them at sea and under musket fire all surrendered! They were examined and put in irons in the local tolbooth.

Captain Smith some time at this point met with a strange young girl called Bessie Millar. Bessie was from Stromness and, although only in her teens, had the locals talking in whispers about her talents as a witch!

Her claim was to be able to sell wind to the fishermen. At a price she could break wind into a captain's hands. With this enriched aroma, he could throw the wind at his boat's sails and with great fortune the wind would take his boat to sea and prosperous fishing grounds!

Over the next eighty years the young Bessie Millar would make her reputation unhindered as a result of the more relaxed attitude towards witchcraft. During the years after 1727, an end came to the witchcraft act that had appeared in Mary Queen of Scots' reign in 1662 – witchcraft was abolished as a capital crime, passed in Parliament by one vote! (1736) Lawyers outvoted church ministers, and for the next hundred years ministers cried into their bibles at what they thought was the unjustness and ungodliness of losing the opportunity to murder 'witches'. In this period of calm, away from the madness of the witchhunts, Bessie made her reputation.

Before Captain Smith paid for his wind he decided to attack and raid a mansion on nearby Isle of Eday where a Mr Mc Fea lived. The decision to attack the mansion was a bold but rash idea. Mr Fea was one of the Orkney baillies and had news of Captain Smith and his remaining crew's whereabouts and had already laid a trap for them.

The pirates were caught just as they were landing to carry out the attack, by the armed coastguard and militia. They were heavily outgunned and had no option but to surrender to Mr Fea's forces. Transported to London in irons on board the man o' war the *Greyhound*, the pirates were taken to the dreaded prison of Marshalsea on the Thames. It was there that they came across their old shipmate, the Welshman Williams, who had arrived in jail just days before! On Wednesday 26th of May 1725, the trial started on the pirates, with Smith changing his name to "Gow" on the charge sheet.

There was no mercy to pirates and the following were given sentences of death: Captain John Smith alias Gow, James Williams, Danial McCawley, Peter Rawlinson, John

Peterson, William Melvin, Robert Winter, James Belvin, and Alexander Rob.

Three men, William Harvey, Robert Teague, and Robert Read, were acquitted.

John Gow at first refused to plead to his charges and was ordered to undergo the sentence of being "pressed to death". Basically he would be tied up and placed under wooden boards, and huge heavy metal weights would be loaded on to him until he died! Under threat of this ordeal, he pled not guilty to the killing of the captain of the seized ship the *Ferneau*, as well as the killing of the captain of the *George*. However he was convicted and awarded death by hanging like his shipmates.

On the 11th of June 1725 all were hanged at Execution Dock in Wapping (as was Alexander Rob a few days later). All the bodies were left to hang in chains as a warning to others.

At Captain Smith's hanging, some of his old crew grabbed on to his legs to hasten his death, the drop not having been sufficient to break his neck. This resulted in the rope snapping, and him being hanged again, till eventually he died!

Years later in 1814, Bessie Millar, now in her nineties and living in a rundown old cottage in Stromness, had a very important and inquisitive visitor: Sir Walter Scott, who was on a recce with thoughts of writing a book on witchcraft. His fellow passenger on his trip to Orkney was his friend J G Lockhart who wrote about the trip and their experiences in his book *Memoirs of the Life of Walter Scott* which was published in 1839. I will give the full experience of meeting the witch Bessie Millar from the pages of the book...

Stromness is a little, dirty straggling town which cannot be traversed by a cart or even by a horse, for there are stairs up and down, even in the principal streets. We paraded its whole length like turkeys in a string, I suppose to satisfy ourselves that there was a worse town in the Orkneys than the metropolis, Kirkwall. We climb, by steep and dirty lanes, an eminence rising above the town, and commanding a fine view. An old hag lives in a wretched cabin on this height and subsists by selling winds. Each captain of a merchantman, between jest and earnest, gives the old woman sixpence, and she boils her kettle to procure a favourable gale. She was a miserable figure; upwards of ninety, she told us, and dried up like a mummy. A sort of clay-coloured cloak, folded over her head, corresponded in colour to her corpselike complexion. Fine light-blue eyes and nose and chin that almost met, and a ghastly expression of cunning, gave her quite the effect of Hecate. She told us she remembered *Gow the pirate* who was born near the House of Clestrom. He came to his native country in 1725, with a *snow* which he commanded, and carried off two women from one of the islands, and committed other enormities. At length, while he was dining in a house in the island of Eda, the islanders, headed by Malcolm Laing's grandfather, made him prisoner, and sent him to London, where he was hanged...We left our

Pythoness, who assured us there was nothing evil in the intercession she was to make for us, but that we were only to have a fair wind through the benefit of her prayers. She repeated a sort of rigmarole which I suppose she had ready for such occasions and seemed greatly delighted and surprised with the amount of our donation. Bessie Millie's habitation is airy enough for Æolus himself, but if she is a special favourite with that divinity, he has a strange choice...On board at halfpast three, and find Bessie Millie a woman of her word, for the expected breeze has sprung up.

Its with this information from J G Lockheart that the pirate Captain Smith should have paid handsomely for his wind and taken his chances on the full sails promised rather than raid the baillies house!

Chapter 14

The Aberdeen Slave Market

If you are a Scotsman living in England for as long as I did, you grow a staunch pride in your country's achievements, almost defence-like in your posture. This is even stronger when you hear your own town being mentioned, a puffing out of the chest, and for all your town's sins, you will verbally defend the place of your birth.

With our next chapter I go to the granite city of Aberdeen in the days before the upheaval of the '45 rebellion and discover an unbiased view of life there from an English officer who was posted there before the troubles started. This is to give background before introducing the main story. This chapter may seem alien to most and it was very surprising to unravel...Aberdeen's lucrative white slave trade!

A description of Aberdeen in 1745...by James Ray, volunteer under the Duke of Cumberland.

> New Aberdeen is situated near the sea and is the capital of the Sherriffdom of Aberdeen...The air is very wholesome, and the inhabitants well bred. There are great quantities of salmon caught here, which the proprietors pickle and export to London. There is likewise plenty of all sorts of white fish. The streets are well paved and the houses built with stone and slate, generally four storeys high. The

town consists of three or four good streets – that called Broad Street is the principal, and is really a fine street of stately houses. There is likewise a fine market-place called Castle Street, which is very spacious, in the middle of which stands an ancient curious Cross, with many antique figures round the upper part of it...Opposite to the Market Cross is the Tolbooth, which serves for a prison...There are three churches...There are two Episcopal meeting houses...The greatest ornament of the city is its College, called the Marischalian Academy, being founded by George Keith, Earl of Marischal, in the year 1593. It has...a good library...The city is built upon three hills but the greatest part is upon the highest, at the head of which stands an old castle, mostly in ruins...The manufacture here is chiefly stockings all round the adjacent country...for exportation to London, Hamburg and Holland...They have an exportation of pork, which they pickle and pack up in barrels, and send to the Dutch for victualling their East India ships. The Aberdeen pork has the reputation of being the best cured in Europe for keeping on long voyages...This town being pleasantly situated, I used to ride out here, after taking a turn to the sea-side over the Links...at the mouth of the river Dee...to observe the ships in the river.

It is against this background of couthy development and modernisation that steps forward our Aberdeen resident Peter Williamson, and his story shows that behind the scenes of this up-to-date and thriving town the town elders were busily involved in the lucrative but secret and dirty business of press-ganging its own citizens. Young men were mugged, kidnapped, and taken to pastures new, taken by force off the streets of Aberdeen and sold into servitude on the plantations of America, if they survived the six week journey. Meanwhile the elders of the town, Baillie William Fordyce, Walter Cochran the town clerk, Alexander Mitchell and others, shared out the price of white slaves amongst themselves.

Every art of deceit was used to lure unsuspecting victims: bribes, alluring promises, and intoxication. Violent press gangs seized Aberdeen residents who seemed fit for the purpose. In the dead of night children would vanish, taken by force from their very own beds. Some of the poorest families sold their own offspring for alms. One account still available to be seen gives these damning figures on what was paid out for receiving live bodies...

To Robert Ross for listing his son, one shilling.
To Maclean, for listing his brother, Donald, one shilling and sixpence.

The victims, once in possession of the oppressors, were driven like flocks of sheep in the night through the town under the care of armed guards to the waiting sailing ships.

The public workhouse and the Tolbooth prison were emptied; some ships were recorded as carrying as many as sixty-nine persons. In the six years from 1743 during which this business was carried on, no less than 600 people were estimated to have been exported by force, travelling as human cargo. Their destiny was to be indentured servants in the plantations of America. Once sold they were officially to become slaves for five to seven years till they recovered the freedom they should never have lost.

During their period of slavery, they were often beaten and whipped, treated with harshness and utter cruelty. For escape attempts, another year of slavery would be added to their lot!

One such victim plucked from the streets of Aberdeen was Peter Williamson, described as "a rough, ragged, humle-headed, long, stowie, clever boy". He was lucky enough to be sold for about £16 to a good master, who in his youth had been similarly kidnapped, in Perth. After many strange reverses in fortune and much adventure by land and sea, through peace and war, Williamson found himself in 1757 in the English port of Plymouth, finally discharged from the British army regiment into which he had been conscripted in America after his release from servitude in the plantations.

His regiment released him from service with a wound and his service money of six shillings. Williamson reached York, and settled down to write his memoirs, which bore the long title: *French and Indian cruelty exemplified in the life and various vicissitudes of fortune of Peter Williamson, a disbanded soldier*.

The book sold well, bringing him much needed prosperity, so that he could at last afford to travel back to Aberdeen to see his parents, in 1758. He travelled in the dress and arms of a "Red Indian" and his book met with great success, applauded wherever he went. He attempted to criticise the authorities for his treatment and was brutally taken by the Sheriff of Aberdeen, who was unimpressed with the edition of his written works damning the Aberdeen authorities. He was convicted of the charge of libel. His books were gathered and publicly burnt at the market cross in Aberdeen centre, by the hands of the local hangman.

Peter was jailed until he signed a denial of the truth of his statements and paid a fine of ten shillings. Finally he was banished from the city. The city chief's wrath was severe, but Peter sought action against the Corporation for these proceedings and won his case! On the 5th of February the court unanimously awarded him £100 damages and another £80 for his legal costs to be paid personally by the defendants.

It was now the intention of the government officers to prosecute the Aberdeen chiefs for their illegal trade of kidnap and slavery, but it appeared that they were covered by an Act of Indemnity.

Peter Williamson raised another action against them and in 1768 received a further £200 in damages from the guilty Aberdeen leaders...William Fordyce, Walter Cochran, and Alexander Mitchell. The compensation for his legal costs was raised to one hundred guineas, or £105. From this date, the lucrative business of the slave trade was crushed in Aberdeen. It may be noted that the money found and brought to Peter Williamson did not come directly from the Aberdeen chiefs' own pockets...it was taken from the coffers of the city.

The following is an extract from Peter Williamson's own memoirs...

Know, therefore, that I was born in Hirnley, in the parish of Aboyne and County of Aberdeen, North Britain, of not rich yet of respectable parents, who supported me in the best manner they could, as long as they had the happiness of having me under their inspection; but fatally for me, and to their great grief, as it afterwards proved, I was sent to live with an aunt at Aberdeen. When under the years of pupilarity, playing on the quay with others of my companions being of stout robust constitution, I was taken notice of by two fellows belonging to a vessel in the harbour, employed (as the trade then was) by some worthy merchants of the town, in that villainous and execrable practice called kidnapping – that is, stealing young children from their parents, and selling them as slaves in the plantations abroad. Being marked out by these monsters of impiety as their prey, I was cajoled on board the ship by them, where I was no sooner got, than they conducted me between the decks to some others they had kidnapped in the same manner. At the time I had no sense of the fate that was destined for me, and spent the time in childish amusements with my fellow sufferers...

When I arrived back in Aberdeen in June 1758 after having completed the period of my slavery...no sooner had I offered this little work to sale in that town, which was then my only means of subsistence, than I was arraigned in a summary complaint at the instance of the Magistrates, before their own tribunal, and carried by four town officers to the bar of that tremendous court of judicature. The complaint exhibited against me contained in substance, "That I had been guilty of causing print, and of publishing and dispersing this scurrilous and infamous libel, reflecting greatly upon the character and reputations of the merchants in Aberdeen, and on the town in general, without any ground or reason; whereby the Corporation of the City, and whole members thereof, were greatly hurt and prejudiced: And that, therefore, I ought to be exemplarily punished in my person and goods; and that the said book and whole copies thereof, ought to be seized and publicly burnt."...

Banished from the capital of the country wherein I was born, and stript of my all, I now bethought myself where or how to apply for redress. In this view I pursued my journey to Edinburgh, but ignorant of the law, and unacquainted with any of its members, equally destitute of money and friends and labouring under the reflections which the calumnious advertisement published by the Magistrates threw on my character, I was utterly at a loss to whom and in what manner I should apply for direction. From this dilemma, however, I was soon relieved by the assistance of kind Providence, who threw me in the way of a gentleman versant in law – a gentleman of knowledge, character, and integrity, by whose advice I was conducted, and by whose advice I was supported, from the infancy to the conclusion of my process. On a fair relation of my grievances, the injuries that I suffered appeared to him so flagrant that he did not hesitate a moment to declare his opinion, that I was not only entitled to ample damages from my persecutors, but that the Court of Session would find no difficulty to award these, with full costs of suit…a process of oppression and damages was commenced, at my instance, against the Magistrates of Aberdeen.

Once the legal necessities had been drawn up against the Aberdeen chiefs, a letter of reply came back to the Edinburgh court with complete ignorance being blamed for the years of the slave trade in Aberdeen. One of the clerks, Walter Cochrane, was given the sole blame for the transportation of boys to America, with the council maintaining that the costs should not come out their pockets as they had no knowledge of the trade. "None of us knew"!

I have the Aberdeen Baillies' letter below.

Aberdeen, February 4, 1764

Sir, – We are sorry to find by yours of 30th past, that there is a sentence pronounced against us in Williamson's process, whereby we are decerned to pay him a very large sum out of our private pockets.

We think it necessary to inform you that our

conduct and intentions, with regard to our sentence against him, have been entirely misunderstood. We can, with the greatest integrity, declare that, at the time of pronouncing that sentence, neither of us knew, directly or indirectly, that Walter Cochrane, the depute clerk, was any way concerned in transporting boys to America, or that there ever was in being the book he produced in proof; that neither of us had ever any interest or concern in such trade; that we never knew, and did not believe, that any men and boys were ever transported from Aberdeen to America contrary to law; that we considered the paragraph in Williamson's book, respecting the merchants of Aberdeen, to be a very calumnious and reproachful aspersion on them which they did not deserve; that Williamson himself had the appearance of an idle stroller, and could give no account of himself, and had produced this pamphlet to be composed for him, of such shocking circumstances, in order the more easily to impose upon, and draw money from the credulous vulgar; and, upon the whole, that we had no motive or interest, either on our own account or any person whatever, or any prejudice against Williamson (having never seen nor heard of him) to induce us to pronounce the sentence against him; that we did it purely, as we judged material justice to vindicate the character of those we believed to be innocent and were unjustly reflected upon; and that, whatever in the sentence appears to their Lordships to be either oppressive or illegal, proceeded entirely from error in judgement, and not from any sinister design; so that, however far the sentence has been wrong, we are ready most freely to make any declaration that may be necessary, that it proceeded from the most innocent intention.

Under these circumstances you will easily perceive how much we are surprised in reading yours, giving an account of the sentence against us; and how hard a thing it is to be decerned to pay a sum of money, as a fine, for doing what we considered to be our duty.

We are, etc.
W Davidson
James Jopp

The letter reeks of rats leaving a sinking ship...Peter Williamson had been admonished in public to the point that the whole city knew of his "crime". Pleading ignorance and blaming the whole deal on a minor officer of the court was nothing but cowardice. Peter declared them "those monsters who made a traffic of the persons and liberties of their fellow creatures".

A further villainous act from this head of Aberdeen council is that following the award of £100 damages on 5th Feb 1762 the councillors succeeded in putting the case to arbitration. Baillie Fordyce and others got the arbiter of the case so drunk that they were able to get the intoxicated arbiter to sign a decision in their favour.

In this deplorable action they were successful, but the

supreme court on the 27th Feb 1766 reversed it. The arbiter it seems was heavily entertained, and is on record as having "a bottle and a half of Malaga, a large dose of spirits, white wine and punch, a mug of porter and two bottles of claret with a mutchkin and a half of rum made into punch."

After that lot, I am surprised he was able to lift a quill and sign anything! After pronouncing judgement, he retired to bed, and lay all the next day (which was Sunday) "dead drunk and speechless". But what a bunch of rogues were running Aberdeen council!

Further reading

Life of Peter Williamson...*Antiquarian Gleanings*... Gavin Turreff, 1859, p. 226

Chapter 15

Captain John Paul of Kirkbean

Every now and then this country of Scotland produces a son who stands proudly in our history. The Wallace, the Bruce, Generals Montrose and Leven, Admiral Wood and Lord Cochrane...and to this number must be added Captain John Paul Jones. Albeit the man did for a while distinguish himself in the colours of Britannia, he excelled in spectacular fashion under the flags of other colours – the flags of revolutionary America, and tsarist Russia.

Born on 6 July 1747 and educated in the parish of Kirkbean in Kirkcudbright, on the west coast of Scotland, John was brought up near the Solway Firth and was soon discovered to have a lasting fascination with the sea. His parents were John Paul, a humble gardener to Mr Craik of Arbigland, and Jean Duff. At twelve years of age the boy was apprenticed to a Mr Younger of Whitehaven, a man heavily engaged in the shipping trade with the American colonies.

John Paul's first voyages were long and laborious six week affairs across the wild Atlantic Ocean, but he took everything in his stride. It seemed he had a destiny of life on the oceans.

After a few years, with a certificate of good conduct, he went aboard the *King George* of Whitehaven, a ship involved in the transportation of slaves. In 1766 he was taken on as third mate, quite a quick rise up the ranks for a nineteen-year-old, but he soon saw the reality of his human cargo's condition. Aghast and disgusted by their suffering, he was to abandon this project quickly, and next took up on a merchant trader called the *John* of Kirkcudbright.

This ship was run by Captain MacAdam, and on his first voyage the captain and his son, who was mate on the ship, both died! Finding himself on his own in control of the ship, John Paul delivered its cargo and brought the ship back safely to Scotland with a firm hand and the confidence of a man twice his age and experience of the seas. It was this event that would see him rewarded by Currie, Beck and company (the ship owners) as ship master of their organisation.

Within a year he moved again, this time to a merchant shipping company in London and command of the *Betsy*, a Caribbean-bound trader. Now he spent a lot of time in the islands of the West Indies, and in 1773 he settled for a while in Virginia to oversee the estate of his brother, who had died suddenly of disease, with no wife or children to hand the house down to. John Paul oversaw the transfer of the property to himself.

When he was twenty-eight years old, the American revolutionary war started against the United Kingdom. Owning property in his adopted country and feeling righteous in the proclamation of freedom and justice, he offered his services to America, changing his name to "John Paul Jones". His services were eagerly accepted by the young republic of America, and from this date he owned no other country.

In the infant navy of America there were three classes

of lieutenant. Jones was placed in the first class position on the 7th of December 1775 and assigned aboard the *Alfred*, and then the *Ranger*, an eighteen-gun warship.

His first voyage to France under the American flag brought two British merchant ships as prizes. He next sailed from the French port of Brest on the 10th

John Paul Jones in American service.

of April towards the Mediterranean and captured another British vessel in the sea off Sicily, raiding its goods then sinking the ship. Next on the 17th another ship fell to him, the *Lord Chatham*, bound for London. It was clear that no British merchant ship was safe in any waters now. John Paul Jones was in Scottish waters next, off Galloway sinking a grain merchant ship, and then another ship from Dublin was also sunk.

The British were soon alerted to a shark in their own waters and battleships were now a constant presence on the coastlines. John Paul Jones went to Whitehaven and observed over 170 boats at rest in the harbour. He started a fire with tar barrels, and before long pandemonium broke out as many ships caught fire. The fortifications there had at least thirty cannons, but as the British tried to bring the guns round to fire them at the American ship in their harbour, they discovered that their guns had been already sabotaged by John Paul Jones with a landing party. This was brilliant, brave stuff and again showed the British that no ship was safe...not even in their own harbours.

John Paul Jones even landed himself near his old home town of Kirkcudbright and raided the local sheriff's own house, stealing all the silverware!

Confrontation with a British man of war was now inevitable, and the British warship the *Drake* was first to confront the *Ranger*. On the morning of the 24th April off the coast of Carrickfergus the ships met and the *Ranger* gave a full broadside from its guns. The battle lasted an hour and five minutes and by the end the *Drake* had her fore and topsails blown away, her sails and rigging cut to pieces and her hull very much damaged. She called for quarter and became Jones's first warship prize.

Only two men aboard the *Ranger* had been killed, while the *Drake* had her captain and thirty of her crew killed, and one hundred and sixty taken prisoner. It was quite a feat, the *Drake* having twenty cannons to the *Ranger*'s sixteen.

The *Ranger* offloaded the prisoners at Brest, and Jones received a frigate of forty guns called the *Duras* which he changed to *Le Bonhomme Richard*. He now had a flotilla of ships under the American flag: the *Alliance* had 36 guns, the *Pallas* had 32, and the *Serf* had 18. In total he had around two thousand men at his command with two further privateers who were promised rewards from any future prizes that were taken.

On the 23rd of August his fleet was seen off the coast of Ireland at Ballinskelligs, County Kerry, where a British man o' war of 22 guns called the *Tartar* intercepted them, sharing broadsides for an hour with one of the ships. Jones's fleet came to assist in the engagement, and the *Tartar* withdrew from action and sailed out of reach.

The fleet worked its way north to Shetland taking a small fishing boat and four of its crew captive. Next, working their way down the east coast they were reported off the headland of Pittenweem putting the town baillies into a panic on the 16th of September. Jones's intention was to burn the naval port of Leith and sink any resistance. An amusing instance happened here when the Pittenweem chiefs sent a boat out. Thinking his squadron was British, they begged for the loan of a cannon or two and powder so they could defend themselves against "the dreaded pirate Paul Jones should he appear and make an attempt on the Pittenweem harbour"!

Captain Jones found this hilarious, and duly sent the Pittenweem chiefs a cask of gunpowder with a note apologising for not sending cannon and shot, but politely saying he had no interest in sacking the town. The barrel, it is reported, was deposited in the cave in Cove Wynd called today "St Fillan's Cave".

At this time, with his fleet sailing to harass Leith, a huge storm broke, sinking one of his support ships and blowing the squadron out of the Firth of Forth. It was noted that many of his ships had bare sails due to this heavy storm. His fleet was as weakened as it had ever been by this mishap, but there was no British ship in the area to confront him and take advantage of the situation.

The fleet was sailing up the east coast of Scotland from

here on the 23rd September 1779 when he came across the British Baltic fleet, homeward bound. Captain Pearson of the British warship *Serapis* came within pistol shot of Paul Jones's flagship and "demanded his ship's name and country or they would open fire". An evasive silence came from within and served for an answer. Then a single cannon shot was answered by a British broadside!

A letter describing the engagement was written by Captain Paul Jones to Benjamin Franklin, then the American Minister in Paris. It was published in the *Scots Magazine* in 1779, I give the full account in the Captain's own words...

"...As we approached the enemy, with our sails out, I made the signal for the forming the line of battle; but with all my eagerness to bring about an engagement, I could not come up with the Commodores' vessel till near seven in the evening. When I came within pistol-shot, he hailed the *Bonhomme Richard*; which I answered with a complete broadside. The engagement immediately commenced, and was carried on on each side with equal violence and fury, each party using the while every possible manoeuvre to work himself into the most advantageous position for annoying the enemy. I am compelled to acknowledge that the enemy's vessel, by various manoeuvres, infinitely superior to those of the the *Bonhomme Richard*, gained sometimes the advantage of situation, in spite of every effort I could make to the contrary. Being engaged with an enemy very much my superior, I found myself under a necessity of being as close as I could, to compensate as much as possible for the inferiority of my strength. My intention was to place the *Bonhomme Richard* plump in front of the enemy's vessel: but as this operation required much address in the manner of managing and governing our sails, and as some of our yard-arms were by that time gone, I could not succeed in this scheme in the full extent I at first intended. The bowsprit of the enemy happening, however, to come within a little of the stern of the *Bonhomme Richard*, I availed myself of this opertunity to fasten the two vessels together; and the wind at the same time upon the enemy's ship, having her stern plump abreast of the *Bonhomme Richard*, the two ships met, almost in all their parts, their yards blended with each other, and the mouths of their cannon respectively touched the decks of each vessel. It was about eight in the evening when this circumstance took place. At this time the *Bonhomme Richard* had received several eighteen pounders under water, and consequently leaked considerably. My battery of twelve-pounders, upon which I built most, being served by French and American sailors, were entirely silenced and abandoned. As for the six old eleven-pounders which formed the battery of my first deck, they did me little service: they only fired eight times in all; and at their being first fired two of them burst, and killed almost all the men appointed for their service.

Before this, Col. de Chamillard, who

commanded a party of twenty soldiers placed on the poop, had abandoned his post, after having lost all his men except five.

I had now only two nine-pounders that were in condition to fire; Mr Mease, the purser, who had the charge of the guns on the poop, having received a dangerous wound on the head, I was obliged to officiate in his stead. I had a great difficulty in rallying some of our men; but having succeeded in drawing our cannon from the leeward battery, we now had three nine-pounders to play upon the enemy. During the whole engagement, the fire from this small battery was seconded only by that of our men from the masts, where Lieut. Stock commanded. I directed the fire of one of the three cannon, charged with bullets, against the enemy's main-mast; while the two others, which were well supplied with case shot, were employed in endeavouring to silence their musketry, and clear their decks; which they at last effected. I learn, that at this instant the enemy was upon the point of asking quarter, when the cowardice or perfidy of three of my subaltern officers induced them at the same time to ask it of the enemy. The English commander asked me if I demanded quarter; and upon being answered in the most determined manner in the negative, the combat was renewed with redoubled fury. They were not able to keep their decks; but the fire of their cannon, particularly of their lower tier, consisting of entirely of eighteen

Battle between *USS Bonhomme Richard* and *HMS Serapis*.

pounders, was incessant. Both vessels were on fire in several places, and the spectacle which they exhibited was frightful beyond description. In order to account in some measure for the timidity of the subaltern officers, that is to say of the master, carpenter, the head gunner and the captain of the soldiers, I ought to observe, that the two first were dangerously wounded; and as the ship had received several shot below water, so that they were obliged to keep pumping almost incessantly, the carpenter was apprehensive of her sinking, in which opinion the two others concurring, the head gunner ran, without my knowledge, to the poop, in order to strike the flag: happily for me, a shot long before had done the office in carrying away the ensign, so that he was obliged to call for quarter. During all this time the *Bonhomme Richard* sustained the engagement alone, and the enemy's ship being far superior in force, could easily have disengaged herself at first, as appeared by their own acknowledgement; and which they could have effected at last, had I not taken care to lash it firmly to the *Bonhomme Richard*. At length, between nine and ten in the evening, the *Alliance* appeared, and I concluded the engagement at an end, when, to my great astonishment, she fired a broadside in the rear of our ship. We then intreated them for God's sake to desist:– she nevertheless continued her fire. We then threw out signals, three lanthorns in a horizontal line, one in the front, one in the rear, and one in the middle of the ship. We all cried with one voice to inform them of their mistake. But nothing had any effect: she passed us, still continuing firing; one of her broadsides killed eleven of my best men, and wounded a good officer. My situation was now deplorable indeed: the *Bonhomme Richard* received several shots below water from the *Alliance*; the pumps were not sufficient to carry out the water; and the flames kept increasing on board the two vessels. Some officers, of whose courage and integrity I had no doubt, attempted to persuade me to yield; the Captain, unknown to me, released all the prisoners; and it must be confessed my prospect began to be truly dreadful; but I was determined not to submit. The enemy's main mast begin to totter, the fire on board their ship began to abate, while on the contrary, ours gained ground. At last, however, between ten and eleven in the evening their ship struck her colours. The ship was the *Serapis* man of war, commanded by the brave Commodore Pearson, a new vessel, mounting 44 guns, built in the new style, having two batteries, the lowest of which consisted entirely of eighteen-pounders.

I had now remaining two enemies yet more formidable than the English, fire and water. The *Serapis* was attacked only by the first, but my ship was assailed by them both. There was six feet of water in the hold; and though the wind was moderate, we could hardly, with the three pumps we had left, prevent it from increasing; while the fire, in spite of all our efforts, extended itself till it reached the powder-room. I caused the powder to be carried upon deck, that it might be ready to throw overboard...

Although John Paul was determined to keep the *Bonhomme Richard* afloat if possible, he had to admit defeat:

"...on the morning of the 25th it appeared plainly impossible to hinder this good ship from going to the bottom. The men did not abandon it till nine o'clock. The water then rose to the upper deck, and a little after ten, with a concern which no words can express, I entirely lost sight of her. No person perished with the vessel, but it was impossible to save any of the provisions..."

The "meteor flag" of England had been lowered to this bold adventurer but his own ship was so damaged in the fight, that he was forced to abandon her. Although the English ship was not in much better condition, he raised his flag on board the *Serapis*, rigged up jury masts, and succeeded in taking her, along with the other prizes, in to the Texel (in the Netherlands).

Captain Jones made haste to a French port where the ships were repaired and British prisoners were exchanged for French and American. He received the thanks of the American ambassador, Dr Benjamin Franklin, for giving liberty to Americans languishing in English jails.

Towards the end of 1780, another confrontation in his new vessel the *Ariel* with a British warship of 20 guns in the Irish channel brought a victory and another prize.

He next sailed back to America where the King of France had recognised his services by presenting him with a superb gold-hilted sword and a letter from the French ministry to the American President requesting permission to "decorate the brave officer Captain Jones with the cross of the order of merit". The letter was laid before the Continental Congress and the proposal was passed on 27 February 1781. A vote of thanks was given for the zeal and prudence and intrepidity with which he had sustained the honour of the American flag, for his bold and successful enterprises to redeem from captivity those citizens of America who had fallen under the power of the enemy and in general for the good conduct and eminent service by which he had added lustre to his character, and to the arms of America. As the war carried on there was no further opportunity for Captain Jones to distinguish himself.

In 1789 he was involved in a diplomatic mission to

Denmark, and he stopped for a while with his wife in Paris. It was there that he was solicited by agents of Russia to take full command of the fledgling Russian fleet anchored in the Black Sea. At first he declined the attractive offer, but was eventually persuaded by the Empress Catherine herself after she sent a personal invitation to visit her in Petersburg. He was invested with the rank of Vice Admiral and took the fleet which was stationed at the Dnieper Estuary, known as the Liman. He took command of the fleet 26 May 1788 on board his flagship *Vladimir*. Military matters were under way with an attack on the Turkish Ottoman Empire at the town of Ochakov.

The Turks had an impressive fleet and attacked the Russians, who would have been destroyed had not Admiral John Paul arrived with his fleet to send the Turks into confusion and they left the scene of battle with great loss. This action occurred on the 4th of June, and for his service he received more honours, the great order of St Anne.

On the 26th of May the whole Turkish Navy attacked Captain Jones's fleet, the battle was fought at the entrance of the Liman where the Turkish fleet was bested and defeated. The flagship of the Turks was taken with eight other capital ships and 4,000 prisoners. The Imperial Gazette of St Petersburg in Russia described the victory as having been gained by Prince Charles of Nassau-Sieger. Furious at someone stealing his hard work and glory, John Paul wrote letters of disapproval to Prince Potemkin in person. It was this action that prompted him to leave in disgust in August 1789.

He retired from service with his wife to Paris where,

on the 18th of July 1792, he became ill with "water in the chest" and died later the same month. He was 45 years old.

In his home country of Scotland, he was known as a rebel and pirate, with his name used to terrify infants along Scotland's coastline. As the laws relative to Calvinists or heretics in France were not abolished at the time of John Paul's death an application was made to the National Assembly. As this was being discussed, his body was pickled in a barrel of alcohol in the hope that the United States of America would pick up their fallen former hero...but no...no one bothered!

A letter to his sister Janette Taylor, from Colonel Samuel Blackden gives some details...

> His body was put into a leaden coffin on the 20th [July], that in case the United States, whom he had so essentially served, and with so much honour to himself, should claim his remains, they might be more easily removed.

But his body was never claimed! It was eventually buried in Paris in St Louis cemetery, which was later closed down. The cost of the interment (462 francs) was paid personally by Pierre-Franç ois Simonneau, the official appointed by Louis XVI to oversee foreign protestant burials in Paris. This was at the height of the French Revolution – Louis XVI was guillotined a few months later, in January 1793.

The body of John Paul Jones lay undiscovered for 113 years, until an American patriot called Horace Porter traced the grave and had it unearthed in 1905.

President Theodore Roosevelt of the USA ordered four battleships to escort the body of John Paul Jones back to America. The ships *Brooklyn*, *Tacoma*, *Chattanooga*, and *Galveston* proceeded to escort the important remains to Annapolis, landing on 23 July 1905.

With great ceremony the body was interred in the crypt at the Naval Academy there. It was seen that the embalming process and preparation of the body was so effective that the body was perfectly preserved, as the photo of his body in 1905 still matched a painting of him from 1785.

John Paul Jones' body in 1905, and his tomb
at U.S. Naval Academy.

Further Reading

The Scots Magazine...1779...letter to Benjamin Franklin

Guide to the East Coast of Fife...D Hay Flemming, 1886...p. 95.

Handy book of the Fife coast...Henry Farnie, 1880..p. 2

Chapter 16

Vincenzo Lunardi
the Lunatic Balloonist

France – the Bois de Boulogne in Paris, on the 21st November 1783. The crowd in the grounds of the Château de la Muette pushed and swayed as they jostled for the best view. To their amusement, men were struggling before them under a cloud of heavy smoke, created by burning damp straw and rags.

Recent months had seen a number of experimental balloon flights. In August, Jacques Alexandre Charles had sent up an unmanned hydrogen balloon, which had landed in Gonesse where brave peasants had chased it and attacked it – killing the flying demon with pitchforks. The Montgolfier brothers, Joseph and Etienne, had developed a balloon lifted by hot air, which in September had carried animals aloft. They had even made a tethered flight with a man, Jean-François Pilâtre de Rozier, on board. Now they had permission to launch a balloon on an untethered flight carrying two pilots – or passengers – Pilâtre de Rozier and François Larent, Marquis d'Arlandes.

The filling of the balloon with hot air had made slow progress, but the process had continued until from the ground arose a massive balloon with a volume of 900 square metres. This great wonder was finally released from its ropes and rose off the ground.

The world's first ever manned hot air balloon flight was under way. Its creators watched it rise, and the awed crowds cheered and screamed. A wonder of invention, it travelled ten kilometres to descend slowly as the heated air cooled. It landed to the south east in the Butte aux Cailles.

A Scottish physician and editor of the *Encyclopaedia Britannica*, James Tytler, inspired by the French balloonists, now used his savings to put himself to the test, experimenting to see if his own balloon could take a man into the air.

From Tytler's own account of his efforts, we learn that he was hindered in raising his "Edinburgh Fire Balloon" by a strong west wind, which blew during the first week of August. It seems that he had a gallery (some kind of platform) and a stove underneath the balloon. But on the Friday evening the gallery caught fire and some of the chains suspending the stove broke. On the next day the balloon was inflated, and Tytler was about to step into the gallery, now in poor condition, when a gust of wind deflated and damaged the balloon. He decided to remove the torn paper lining the balloon, and varnish it instead. However the gallery had now been put out of action, and so the stove, which weighed 135 kilograms, could not be carried up with the balloon.

I now came to the resolution of suffering myself to be projected into the air by inflating the Balloon to the utmost, and being appended to it without any furnace, like a log or piece of ballast. You will easily see that this was the resolution of a *madman*, and which nothing but my desperate situation could excuse.

One fine morning in August 1784, he exposed the freshly varnished balloon to a strong heat for an hour or so. Sitting in a basket used to carry pottery, he let himself be lifted off the ground. The ascent was stopped by a rope fixed to a mast that held the balloon up during inflation. People also held the balloon down, which stopped the ascent, but once it was let go, it shot up "a very small way", estimated at 100 or 150 metres, and then came down with a bump about a kilometre away. "I had scarce time to taste the pleasures of an aerial journey".

Tytler constructed a new stove and gallery, and decided to fly again on the 29th September, but wind and rain prevented this, and the attempt was put off until 11th October. Although he wanted to try a private experiment first, he found more than a thousand people waiting at Comely Garden. Unfortunately, the balloon when inflated could scarcely bear its own weight. In Tytler's opinion, the new stove was too small, but he now found himself insulted and called a cheat, a rascal, a coward and a scoundrel. He had a larger stove constructed, but the weather was still bad, and the balloon was leaking like a sieve. A private experiment failed, and the next thing was that the balloon was seized as part of a claim for damages.

After a legal process of six months, Tytler managed to get the balloon released, but he was now unwell. At last on 26 July 1785 the balloon had been repaired and another attempt was made. A fire had been applied for a mere four minutes before the balloon was damaged by a violent wind and the stove was "dashed in pieces", after which Tytler abandoned his efforts to fly.

Tytler had inner demons. He was once a physician, but his fondness for drink had claimed his business. He became outspoken against his peers and financial backers, eventually being disabled by the courts with writs against him. When he became verbally abusive to the men who held the purse strings supporting his venture, eventually his backers pulled away from his dream and his total bankruptcy followed.

Losing friends and finding himself alienated, he took himself off to America for a new start in life in Salem, Massachusetts. He thought to make a new start for himself with employment as a doctor, but before long his drinking and his bad temper returned and ruined his business once more! On the 9th of January 1804, he left his house, yet again drunk. What exactly happened next is a mystery, but two days later his body was found washed up by the tide.

James Tytler is a forgotten pioneer in ballooning history today, but he paved the way for other pioneers in Scotland, one such being a young Italian called Vincenzo Lunardi!

Lunardi was born in the town of Lucca, in Italy to a wealthy family regarded as minor nobility. His schooling was of the best and it wasn't long till he was working as the secretary to Prince Caramanico who was now the Italian Ambassador to Britain. With this position, he found himself based in London. It was while he was here his attentions were taken by the invention of ballooning.

You needed three things in abundance to continue research in ballooning...

1. Money! This was what the pioneer James Tytler never had, and his lack of funds generated a furious temper which scared off his backers.
2. Bravery!…James Tytler reached 150 metres!…one mistake was certain death!
3. Madness!…James Tytler was known as totally eccentric with bouts of rage and drunkenness.

Lunardi had all three qualities – in abundance.

The Italian had made two successful balloon trips already in London, one lasting two and a quarter hours, travelling 40 kilometres and witnessed by a crowd of 200,000 viewers.

Now he chose Scotland to enhance his work in ballooning. Making his way to Edinburgh, he followed his enthusiasm and before long a balloon bag had been carefully constructed. The amazing tale of his brave struggle as a pioneer of ballooning is captured in his own letters, written to his Italian benefactor and guardian Chevalier Gerardo Compagni. It is from these letters, written in 1785–86, that I get the information of his five attempts of his aerial voyages in Scotland. He obviously regarded James Tytler as a brave failure, because he included Tytler's description of his own experiments with his letters when they were published in his book *An Account of Five Aerial Voyages in Scotland*. But Lunardi wrote that he was inspired by the prospect of becoming "the first Aeronaut in Scotland".

It was with the support of the Duke and Lady Buccleugh that his actions to fulfil his ballooning dream were met with support and enthusiasm from the gentry

Vincent Lunardi

and nobility of Scotland. The glowing public followed him likewise with zeal and sensational adoration whenever he appeared to further the project.

He made the elegant Walkers Hotel in Princes Street his residence and in his letters home he mentions seeing from there "innumerable elegant buildings". His choice of the perfect position to ascend from in his balloon fell into two categories – a high position such as Arthur's Seat or Calton Hill, or George Square in the town surrounded by tall buildings. With his thoughts on wanting his audience in the thousands to see his lift-off he chose George Square. The city chiefs Honourable Henry Erskine, Sir William Forbes, and Major Frazer made sure his requests were granted. In one of his many letters home he states with excitement:

> Scotland cannot boast a happier man than your friend. I can assure you that I rise some inches taller to take in a more extensive view of my delightful prospects!

Such were Lunardi's expectations of imminent success and fame that he asked if several areas of George Square could be fitted with iron railings and enclosed specially as he expected spectators in the thousands. Lunardi proposed the adventure to be ready to take off on the 5th September 1785. But his enthusiasm was severely dented when resistance to his plans was met from a woman who was powerful enough to stop his development in George Square.

Describing her as "a female Machiavel of fifty," Lunardi described her in a quoted poem as

> ...she on whom the wild December pours
> The chilling influence of his icy show'rs, Whose fifty winters have effac'd her charms, And frowning sent her from their shrivell'd arms.

Writing that he had to give up all thought of George Square, he turned his attention to the College, which had an open space that could hold the thousand onlookers Vincent expected for his venture, but an "artist" belonging to the College had already blocked his approach by suggesting that roofs of neighbouring houses might be damaged by the mob. The Infirmary also refused to provide a launch site. His next step, on the Lord Provost's advice, was to try Heriot's Hospital – they at once assented. Lunardi wrote: "Thus, with a little friendly assistance I have surmounted those difficulties which almost warped my brain!"

Vincent started his plans again. Work quickly progressed and a date was set again for lift off. But once again his plans were thwarted by his delivery of chemicals coming from Liverpool.

> I sent my servant, last night, to the place where the waggon puts up, and the Innkeeper told him that I was mistaken; that it required 16 days to come from Liverpool hither, and if the waggoner said

otherwise, it was only in order to secure to himself some emolument from the carriage.

People were travelling from as far as Aberdeen and Glasgow to see the event. Vincent was aggrieved to let so many down who had made such plans to travel. Carrying on with preparations, Vincent set a contract with a plumber Mr Chalmers, to make two separate sealed canisters four metres by one wide to store the gas for the balloon in. The price was £20 for the pair.

The military in Edinburgh now seeing the amount of technical debris scattering the College campus, Colonel Cochran offered some of his men to safeguard the accumulating items.

Further setbacks came when the plumber Chalmers missed the date of completion for the tanks. His contract was ripped up and another called Mr Salby was procured at the same price who managed to produce the goods in good time.

A small cannon was bought to fire and announce his balloon's start of flight! And the date was set for October 7th 1785.

On Wednesday 7th October a massive crowd watched the balloon being filled with gas, taking a slow three hours. The balloon was constructed of eight huge bladders, with 25 kilograms of sand to be used as ballast, several ropes held a basket in place and Vincent wore a cork jacket that could keep him afloat if the balloon came down over water.

At 3.45pm the balloon rose from the College ground to the thrilled cries of the crowd, waving like a lunatic to his fans from above, throwing flowers down as his balloon rose to 350 metres, where he then dropped down a 12-metre flag onto his supporters as they cheered and screamed up to him their adorations.

He could see over the hills of Edinburgh the city of Glasgow and Paisley in the far distance…the balloon was following winds to the northeast which brought him over the sea. He continued now at 600 metres high and thought fearlessly that the balloon would might soar out of sight completely. He saw boats below and slowly reached land again, drifting over Largo Bay in Fife, flying over the villages of Largo where the bemused farmers and workers were deciding if they should shoot at the strange visitation or wave.

He found the contraption was starting to reduce height drastically, so he dropped the first of his bags of sand ballast and reached 150 metres where he entered a cloud, he let go a further 1.5 kilos of sand and rose above the cloud, to his great amusement. The air currents continued the balloon moving north east, but the contraption began to descend alarmingly.

It seemed his good luck was prevailing as at 4.20pm the balloon hit flat farmland near the village of Ceres. Vincent had by this time in flight donned his Italian military uniform and his cork jacket to greet his onlookers, who were farmer Robert Christie and Mr Mathew, keeper of the inn in Cupar. The astonished witnesses explained to Vincent he had landed in Fife, at Ceres near Cupar and took him to the local Council Hall in Cupar. He was treated like a superior being by all lower classes and high society.

As word spread of his incredible journey, multitudes of people descended on Cupar for a glimpse of this hero. He was given the high honour of the freedom of the town by the Cupar Provost. He was entertained by all in a flurry of invitations. The golfing society entertained him, honouring him as a "Burgess of St Andrews". An honorary member of the Royal Archers Company was next, with the "Freedom of the Metropolis" to follow, given by the Lord Provost and Magistrates of St Andrews. He was a week later made a "Burgess of Edinburgh" by the Provost James Hunter, accolades followed from the council chiefs acknowledging his achievement in this honour:

> In testimony of their sense of the undaunted courage of Vincent Lunardi Esq of Lucca, in ascending in a Balloon, and passing the Firth of Forth to Fife with the wind at South West, at the manifest risk of being blown into the German ocean, admitted and received and hereby admit and receive him a Burgess and Guild Brother of the said City.

His accolades kept coming, one such diploma offered to him was from the notorious Anstruther sex club – "The Beggars Benison". Whether he visited the club is unmentioned in the records but Lunardi did have an eye for the ladies. The club made him "A Knight Companion of the most ancient and puissant Order of the Beggars Benison and Merryland".

He took his next balloon trip to Kelso with the support of the gentry there. This time his balloon was bigger in size, 450 metres of silk were used and the contraption once full of his chemicals was shaped like a pear. He rose from the church yard, eventually reaching 1,800 metres, and coming down in a field near the village of Barmoor in Northumberland. Again he was treated admirably by all and more accolades came his way. A further flight was taken in the City of Glasgow from St Andrews Churchyard, on 23rd November. Some bystanders were in tears at his posture as the balloon rose; others, mainly ministers, claimed he was "in compact with the Devil and has been reprobated by the Almighty".

His second attempt at ballooning in the city of Edinburgh had the guns from Edinburgh Castle announce his departure to a crowd of many thousands. But the wind that took his balloon sent his contraption over the Firth of Forth and out towards the German Ocean (North Sea). His balloon lost height and crash landed into the sea a few kilometres from North Berwick, where he floundered in the water until being rescued by a fishing boat crammed full of fish.

His contraption was lost to the waves and sank. Lunardi, in his letters to his Italian benefactor, praised Scottish noblewomen:

> The British women, who fill the higher ranks of life, may, I think, be pronounced the handsomest in Europe! but the case is different with the lower class: this contrast is very striking in Scotland, where the country girls, and those in servile stations, continually go bare-footed.

In all he did five flights in Scotland, and his private

letters home showed his praise for a country that supported him in his exploits, and he was entirely thankful.

He made another balloon flight in England in 1786. This time it took place in Newcastle, but during the balloon's lifting his servant was entwined in the rope. He was lifted to a great height and fell, to die from his wounds a few days later. Lunardi was devastated; he later retired to Portugal and never married, dying in 1806.

Reading Lunardi's letters, I take a great pride in the way my country of birth reacted to his visit, and the support it gave him. A foreigner, of minor nobility from Italy...it had been just forty years before Lunardi's visit, that a similar man of nobility from Italy had caused this country such upheaval, turning father against son in a chain of battles. The result of his failure would cause the Highlands to be depopulated in a forced exodus of immigrants to America...he was called Bonnie Prince Charlie.

Further reading

An account of five aerial voyages in Scotland, in a series of letters to his guardian, Chevalier Gerardo Compagni...Vincent Lunardi, 1786

Vincenzo Lunardi plaque near Ceres, Fife.
The plaque reads:

VINCENZO LUNARDI
BORN IN LUCCA, ITALY, IN 1759, HE ASCENDED
IN A HYDROGEN BALLOON ON 5TH OCTOBER 1785
FROM THE GARDEN OF HERIOT'S HOSPITAL,
EDINBURGH, HE LANDED AT COALTOWN OF
CALLANGE IN THE PARISH OF CERES, HAVING
TRAVELLED 46 MILES. THIS WAS THE FIRST
AERIAL VOYAGE IN SCOTLAND.

Chapter 17

A Hanging Premonition

Aberdeen 1785. The crowd in Marischal Street had been impatiently waiting, and suddenly there was movement. The people crushed forward to get the best view, figures could be seen. With guards on either side, a woman was being brought up the steps of the wooden stage, pathetic, malnourished and looking anxious and confused to why she was there.

All types of the city's citizens were present: vagrants, workers, and here and there soldiers in red uniforms. Today would see the common thief Elspeth Reid make her peace with God and be hanged to death on the scaffold.

She had been caught stealing linen cloths and other women's clothing from washing drying areas. Elspeth was a habitual thief and alcoholic vagabond. Arresting her and jailing her put nothing but expense on the city. From the minute she went over the threshold of a jail cell, she cost money, as did all those who encountered the dark dungeons of the Tolbooth in Aberdeen.

All fines incurred for crimes had to be paid, as did the food, security costs and paperwork incurred in a stay in the Tolbooth. There was no one left who would pay Elspeth Reid's fees and fines any more. She was now utterly friendless. A habitual thief for years, she had been warned by judges and courts that they would not tolerate her arrests any longer, and still she had paid no heed. This new theft brought the harshest of charges against her. She was to be made an example of, and this would rid the city of someone who was nothing but a burden to the public purse. She was sentenced to be hanged by the neck till dead!

Little Catherine Davidson was in her early teens and swept along by the excitement of witnessing a public hanging. She had been there early to command a decent view of the proceedings.

The crowd grew into thousands: it seemed the citizens of Aberdeen had all turned out to see the sorry sight of Elspeth Reid meeting her end on the noose of the hangman's rope! The moment came when Elspeth stood, and she said a few words which the crowd could not hear. The hangman put a hood over Elspeth Reid, pulled a lever fast, a secret trapdoor in the floor opened and she fell straight down, breaking her neck. The crowd cheered as the rope was pulled back up and cut down from the gibbet, the noose was removed from the victim's neck and the hangman taunted the audience with it, waving it like a lasso around his head as the crowd cheered.

He let the noose fly into the crowd as was tradition and the rope slapped down on Catherine Davidson. She caught it square on her chest. For a moment she couldn't hear a thing. The crowd cheered loudly but she saw only open mouths, no noise. It was the strangest of things, as she looked back at the scaffold, she was horrified to see herself there, holding the noose. With the hangman...but he was putting the noose around her neck!

She screamed! Then the vision was gone. She still held the executioner's rope in her hands but was led away by her friends. For the next forty-five years this nightmare would follow her.

Catherine would grow into womanhood, settling in her home town of Aberdeen. She would eventually marry a tavern owner and become Mrs Humphreys. But over the years the tavern would take its toll. Socialising with the customers was a way of life that brought ruin to many a publican. Alcoholism was rife, with wine and beers readily at hand. And so Mr and Mrs Humphreys descended into a gin-soaked existence. Drunken vicious brawls were a hazard of the back-street taverns in Aberdeen, but here it was often as not the tavern owners themselves entertaining the base quality of drinkers, screaming and fighting each other.

Mr Humphreys would joke "that one day his own wife would hang and face Marischal Street herself" meaning in jest – "in one of her drunken rages in the near future, there was every chance she would kill him".

Aberdeen in 1830, with a population of 177,657, had its employment deeply involved in the textile industry. 4,000 people were employed in the business, manufacturing thread, sailcloth, brown linens and sacking. Woollen items like stockings and blankets were much desired and exported to Germany and Holland. The city had 2,000 weavers adding to this. Granite was in great demand (24,000 tonnes shipped) and mined and transported in huge quantities. Salmon and cattle were also in demand.

A workhouse had been formed for destitute boys and girls, in 1739. Its purpose was to rid the city of vagabonds

163

and to contribute to giving the poor children a way out to apprenticeships in the linen trade. It may have been because of the embarrassment of Elspeth Reid's predicament that the charges against her were so severe. The town chiefs had to continue to pump funds into the workhouse to keep it from closing and to meet the needs of the vagrants it supported, as it was not self-sufficient. Elspeth being a beneficiary of the workhouse had disgraced the town's charity and turned to theft.

The linen trade requires the product to be washed in bleaching materials to render the threads soft and clean. Before the 1800s human urine was used, and sometimes sour milk and then citric acid. In the nineteenth century new and economical ways of producing a product called "vitriol" led to it replacing the previous foul-smelling agents and being seen as the definitive product for bleaching the linen. Vitriol, or sulphuric acid, is a mineral acid. It is made by burning sulphur to create sulphur dioxide gas; this is oxidised to sulphur trioxide and dissolved in a hydrogen peroxide solution which produces sulphuric acid or vitriol, a very caustic acid! With Aberdeen in 1830 having such a large linen manufacturing industry, the new bleaching product was readily available, with a vitriol manufacturing plant now based in Prestonpans.

Man has over the centuries never ceased to amaze in the many inventive ways created to kill off his enemies. Killing your husband with vitriol is probably neither the quietest nor the cleanest way to do it! But one drunken night in the Humphrey household, Catherine waited till her husband was in bed. The titanic row that had fuelled this moment of madness spurred her on to pour the caustic vitriol into her sleeping husband's mouth. He erupted in a fountain of blood as the acid burnt into the tissue and muscle of his neck and arteries. He thrashed around in his deathly last moments of despair and pain. Then he lay dead upon the floor as the acid continued to corrupt his face.

The noise of his death brought the authorities and the arrest of Catherine. She was taken to the Tolbooth.

In the magistrates' court that followed, Catherine confessed in answer to a question from the Reverend Ian Murray, saying...

> "I acknowledge the justice of my sentence but...I did not buy the stuff to give him! But misfortune took hold of me and I gave it to him...I did not think it would kill him, but I did it and will suffer justly for it".

Catherine Humphreys was led to the scaffold to be hanged on the 8th October 1830. She was the first woman in 45 years to be hanged in Aberdeen, the first since Elspeth Reid.

On October the 11th, the *Caledonian Mercury* newspaper, published as a broadsheet by John Muir, described the hanging of Catherine. "Since her condemnation she has conducted herself in an exemplary condition" but 45 years previously she had the premonition that this would be her fate, after witnessing the hanging of Elspeth Reid and catching the rope all those years ago.

On the scaffold, she exclaimed, "Oh my God" before the trapdoor opened.

When researching this story for this book I tried to find where exactly Mrs Humphreys had her Tavern. The Gazetteer of Scotland, printed in 1844, gives Aberdeen 193 wine merchants and 41 spirit dealers, but I have found nothing to pinpoint the location.

Further reading

Caledonian Mercury...Mon 1th Oct, 1830

Aberdeen information...The Gazetteer of Scotland, 1844

Chapter 18

Take Your Partners for the St Vitus Dance

Scotland, like many other European countries, had its fair share of plagues and diseases, probably not suffering as much as our English neighbours because our population was spread thinly across large areas. That is not to deny that the capital city of Edinburgh suffered badly, as did St Andrews, losing one third of its clergy to the plague in the 1600s. Doctors and prayers were futile gestures against a tide of rampant death! In London in 1665, 5,000 dead a week were being piled in huge open burial pits. Men and women were wracked in pain from huge black boils appearing in hours from the lymphatic glands of the armpits and between the legs and ran screaming through the town, towards the River Thames to throw themselves to a watery death and end the suffering!

In earlier times, in the border wars of 1340, Scottish troops laughed at the English army being decimated from within, with the plague killing more than Scottish spears could. They called it "the English disease" but their laughter was short-lived as it hit the Scots camps and devastated them also in a tide of death. The ignorant and desperate people of my home village of Largo thought that sentry posts on the outskirts of the area with loaves of bread fixed to high poles would tell of the plague's arrival...the bread going the same colour as the coming boils of death...purple mould being mistaken for the approaching disease.

Ignorance of medical advancement was the church's stance to those who experimented in medicine, accusing its practitioners of witchcraft and ridding themselves of the few who dared to innovate. Trumped up church trials awaited the likes of Alison Pearson in St Andrews in 1588 who used the herbs foxglove and woodruff to heal Archbishop Patrick Hamilton. His thanks for being cured of his many ailments was a burning pyre for her acts of witchcraft! It was this stance which set back medical advancement for 300 years.

In 1799, the completion of the publication of the *Statistical Account of Scotland* proved to be a milestone in the history of the country. It was a detailed survey of every village and town in Scotland, for the first time giving a history of the population at large. It held details of birth and death rates, farming and the inhabitants' lifestyles. The nationwide survey was brought out by Sir John Sinclair and in the Fife volume which I have, it deals with a very strange disease rampant in the small parish of Leuchars near St Andrews. Let me take your hand, if I may, and introduce you to the "St Vitus Dance".

The name Leuchars is derived from an old Celtic language and signifies the description of a wet flat land. In 1799 according to the *Statistical Account*, a very considerable amount of wheat was farmed here; peas and beans were in good measure farmed here too. Everyone who rented land here grew their own potatoes, and there were 1,559 cattle and 420 horses in the area. At least five farms shared the land.

There is an area nearby sitting to the east of Leuchars which again is very flat. It is a forest today on marshland, but it is said to get its name from a Viking fleet that came to grief on the coast here and settled in the safety of this forested area in shelters of tents, as the ground was too boggy to build stone construction. It is from this it gets its name "Tentsmuir" (Tentsmoor).

In 1799, around 1,700 people lived in the area. There was good sanitation, with a water trench cut into the soil leading to the River Eden, where good fishing could be had. It was a clean, windswept area graced by the shadows of kings in the past, this once having been a royal hunting ground of the Stewarts. But a strange disease had surfaced in the 1700s. In the writings of the *Statistical Account*, it was mentioned as having appeared in the population three times in the previous twenty years: 1780–99. It went by the name the "St Vitus Dance" named after the thirteen year-old martyr Vitus, born in Sicily, who was tortured by the Romans to try to get him to renounce his Christian faith in 303 AD. The dead boy's remains were taken to Germany and worshipped there. They would celebrate in front of his relics by dancing!

When a person was infected by "St Vitus Dance" they shook in violent spasms. "It was desired that a fiddle should be played on in the presence of the affected person. It was not regular music that gave relief, but the striking of certain strings, which the person under agitation, desired should be struck again. The effect was astonishing; the person affected, became quiet, sat down, and in a little, asked to be put to bed, but still called for the person to play, till the feelings that produced the agitation were abated." (OSA, Vol XVIII, 1796, pp 606-7)

It was diagnosed as a neurological disorder and named Sydenham's chorea after an English doctor in 1686. Thomas Sydenham described the chorea in his work *Schedula Monitoria de Novae Febris Ingressu* It was associated with rheumatic fever, but not until 180 years later, in 1866. The features of chorea are involuntary movements, hypotonic and muscular weakness. The fluctuating strength of the patient shows fingers moving in a way one would play a piano. The treatment and cure are rest and penicillin.

One of the stranger diseases I've come across and with the violinist on hand to find the right note, it must have been murder for neighbours and families nearby to listen as the patient suffered till the right soothing sound could be produced. As I can tell you, coming from a musical family myself – my younger brother and sister both played the violin. Its torturous tunes can still be remembered, putting me nearly in my own "St Vitus Dance" trance!

Further reading

The fireside book of deadly diseases...Robert Wilkins

Wei F Wang...Images in clinical medicine...Sydenhams Chorea

Statistical accounts of Scotland Fife edition...1799

Chapter 19

The Isle of May Tragedy

It was the last days of January 1791, and a terrible storm was brewing. On the east coast of Fife in winter it starts to get dark roughly about five o'clock, by six or seven you can hold your hand in front of your face and it will be so dark you won't be able to see it without the moon's help. To be at sea, as a fisherman or a mariner, at this period, was an utterly dangerous profession. Between this date and 1880, over 50 ships would go down, wrecked off the east coast here. The islands of the May and the Bass Rock and Bell Rock were hazards that doomed many a ship on their rocky outposts, unseen till too late in the pitch dark. Maps might have shown a feature, but its whereabouts in the darkness was always uncertain.

Lighthouses became the saviours for many. This would be a simple construction burning a large beacon in a brazier of burning coal as a warning for the captains and navigators to look out for. The May Isle was the first working lighthouse in Scotland, built in 1635 by James Maxwell and John Cunningham. A crude but efficient enough structure, it burned over a tonne of coal in its metal brazier every night. Records state that 406 tonnes a year were used here, all extracted from nearby Pittenweem's mines.

One of the architects of the lighthouse would come to a bitter end: he was drowned returning to the fishing port of Anstruther. A local woman Eppie Laing would be charged with his murder by witchcraft and was burned with two unnamed others on the beach walkway in 1643 by the minister David Monroe.

The storm of January 1791 lasted a week, and in that period of violence no boat could venture out the Fife harbours. Boats sat riding out the storm in safe havens as the protective harbour walls took a pounding.

Eventually a relief boat with more supplies of coal and other groceries for the lighthouse made its way over to the May Isle. George Anderson was the keeper at the time, living in the lighthouse with his wife and six children. Ships coming to the east coast harbours had been complaining that no lights were being shown from the brazier. Henry Dowie was in charge of the relief boat; he knew George Anderson to be a reliable man, an able seaman and a good friend.

The May Isle sits at the entrance of the Firth of Forth between the Fife coast and North Berwick coastline. It is 1.6 kilometres by 500 metres wide, a massive bird sanctuary, heaving with wild rabbits and seals basking on the beaches like great sausages on a barbecue. There was a small monastery situated here in the 9th century run by Saint Monan, which was overrun by Viking hordes who weren't shy of carrying out a massacre or two. In this instance they murdered near 300 monks here!

The lighthouse was a sturdy masonry building 7.3 metres wide by 12 metres high. The top of the building was vaulted to hold a flat roof set in a tapered circular fire box 530 mm deep by 850 mm wide. The metal furnace was loaded with a tonne of coal on the ground then hoisted up on chains by a pulley system. The brazier once lit could be seen at sea from five miles away and the light warned captains there were hazards in that area to avoid. It was crude but efficient.

The relief boat approached the island in the now calm waters of the North Sea, but it produced an uncanny silence in the Captain, as usually they would have been spotted

Sketch of the original lighthouse on the Isle of May.

by telescope by now. A welcome party would be preparing for the arrival of new provisions and the Anderson children would be running around the beach.

But strangely there was no movement on the island...nothing stirred but the screaming of gulls...something was amiss. The boat landed in the little natural harbour on the east of the island, tied itself up safely, and as the crew started to unload the ship Henry Dowie made his way up towards the lighthouse. The sun caught the building in silhouette as he approached. It was silent...too silent!

The suspicions of the relief crew were proved too tragically true as they opened the lighthouse entrance and viewed the living quarters of Mr Anderson and his six young children. At first all were seen to be in a deep sleep, tucked up nicely in their beds, but on closed examination they found the unmistakable smell that was of death and disaster! All had perished, all the pretty ones, and mother and the father, dead in their sleep. The constant emptying of the brazier's ashes day after day had resulted in a tremendous build-up of slag. Grey ashes in a huge mound emptied day after day, month after month had built up to a tremendous height. It had caught fire...smouldered away quietly, and as the family slept through the wicked storm outside with door and windows firmly closed, the quiet assassin went to work. Smoke from the burning slag heap had reached in through the ventilation slats built into the lighthouse on high. The sleeping family never stirred as the smoke slowly filled the lighthouse. Invisible fumes poisoned the Anderson family as they slept. All seemed dead. But from this scene of terror something stirred, and a child's whimper was heard...one was alive!

It was the youngest daughter Lucy Anderson and herself not a year old. She was trying to suckle her dead mother. The pale rictus grin of the mother was met by the grin of the youngster on seeing rescue.

Henry Dowie managed to bury the Anderson family on the isle, all together as they were in death. He carefully took the year old Lucy back to Pittenween, where he and his wife brought the wee one up as though one of their own children. During the next 12 years his wife would die, and Henry then married 13 year old Lucy (when a girl reached 12 she was seen old enough to marry)

Then as newlyweds they immigrated to America where they had 12 children.

A relative of the Isle of May survivor Lucy Anderson retraced her family footsteps recently right to the tragedy that took her ancestors.

A new lighthouse was built in 1816. It's this building that remains today. A regular boat service can be had from a shipping company in Anstruther for tourists to explore the Island...the Author highly recommends it as a great day out...but bring waterproofs as you're rather exposed here!

Isle of May, Robert Stevenson's 1816 lighthouse can be seen in the center of the island.

Further Reading

Gazetteer of Scotland, vol. 2...1844

Guide to Pittenweem and St Monans...J,G Innis, 1900

Guide to the East Neuk of Fife...D Flemming, 1886

Key of the Forth...John Jack, 1858

Chapter 20

The Kirkmichael Curling Disaster

I have an energetic friend I have known since school; back then we shared a mutual love of music and the merits of sustained beveraging, sorting the universe's problems in lovely big measures. Twenty years went past as our careers took us to different parts of the country, but when we met again I found that this family man's hobbies now included a fascination for standing stones, mountain climbing and cracking the 300-plus Munros in Scotland,* and that he was in the mad process of conquering them a second time all over again!

Now Stephen Gilfeather is built like a gazelle. He is a mountain goat of a man, as the author can affirm. During a climb up a local near 300-metre vertical landmark in Largo, my lungs were hanging out of my mouth while the human mountain goat hadn't even broken sweat! But he told me statistics of the sport and how dangerous it was. Lightning strikes, exposure, and rock falls are the main causes of death in this sport. His own tales of witnessing death on the mountains on two occasions opened my eyes to the regular fifteen-plus deaths registered each year in Scotland alone.

The statistics led me to a search on our other national sports and the dangers linked to these sporting pastimes.

---

* The Munros are mountains in Scotland taller than 3,000 feet. They are named after Sir Hugh Munro, who surveyed and catalogued them in 1891.

My attention was caught by an instance back in 1813, within the boundaries of Kirkmichael Parish in Dumfriesshire, where one local village had issued a sporting challenge to another in winter, in January when the local Cumrue Loch had frozen over. Lochmaben Parish had issued a challenge to Kirkmichael Parish for a game of curling!

The two parishes had populations of around 1,000 villagers each, according to the Statistical Account of the area gathered in 1790. A typical collection of wheelwrights, blacksmiths, weavers, shoemakers, clogmakers, tailors, carpenters, and millers. They put up notices of the upcoming game, and great interest was taken in each locality as they chose their champions to fight for the village's honour.

The last Saturday in January was picked for the event, with a 2pm start to the game. The loch had been frozen over for weeks, as was usual at this time of year. The Saturday chosen was blessed by sunshine and was as pleasant a day as one could hope for – a day out in the frozen fields by the loch side.

As the curling warriors carried their stones to the place chosen for the game, it was noticed that there was a fair bit of slush on the surface. Some of the best skaters in the area flew gracefully around on the outskirts of the players, impressing the growing numbers of supporters who had turned out in great numbers for the game. One such man gracefully spun a complete circle around the players, driving a slushy wake towards them at which he received an amount of torrid abuse from the splattered and wet players.

The skater smiled at his handiwork and flew off, gliding over the ice on his skates with his back to his victims. He skated another full circle to face his angry villagers with a cheeky smile...but his smile turned to horror, because where the villagers had been standing was now a massive chasm of dark forbidding water! He had skated a full circle around them...and the ice had fallen through at his skates' impression in the ice! Pandemonium ensued, as the drowning curlers fought against heavy waterlogged jackets and jerseys to keep above the frozen waters; arms flailed and heads fought to keep above the frozen waterline.

Flat on the ice lay friends and family, throwing out jerseys and coats as lifelines, while others held their legs in support. There was a ring of bodies around the broken ice, all frantically trying to reach the stricken curlers; a ladder was brought and stretched across the hole in the ice and one curler was pulled from icy death, then another...and another three men. But for five others who fell into the freezing water, rescue came too late: when finally pulled from the loch, life had expired from them.

All the victims were young men, under twenty-three years of age. The dead were...

William McGill, from Corshill

James Patterson, Auchenclurehill

James Dalzell, Parkgate

Robert Muirman, a servant at Dalfibble farm

Peter Carruthers, a servant at Dalfibble farm.

Several newspapers covered the tragedy, the *Scots Magazine* in its issue of February 1813; the *Caledonian Mercury* also in February 1813, and the *Lancaster Gazette* in 1813.

The following write-up is taken from the *Lancaster Gazette*.

> On Saturday last as two persons were skating on Cumrue Loch a parish of Kirkmichael, one of them made a dextrous wheel round a number of spectators who happened to be collecting at one place. The impression of his skates so weakened the thawing ice it instantly gave way and ten persons were plunged into the water when it was 11 feet deep! Five people perished.

In the records in the Statistical Account I have found a wonderful antidote to the malice of hatred that one human being may bear towards a fellow human being, which often results in the discord of many. In the Parish of Kirkmichael there existed a method of solving petty squabbles.

If anyone in the parish had a grievous complaint against a fellow citizen, a friend would gather friends and organise "A Drinking". This would start with the two unhappy citizens together at a table drinking beer and eating bread, this would then be changed to whisky and brandy and over time this would inevitably mean music and dancing and woeful singing. It is recorded that by the end…no one had any troubles!

This unspoken rule Steve and I have practised religiously, and we've been best friends for decades now!

Curling Stone.

Chapter 21

The Shot Colonel of Shotts

On the route of the principal highway between the two cities of Edinburgh and Glasgow, lies the village of Shotts. An unremarkable-looking wee village with an utterly magnificent history.

It has witnessed, in the turmoil of time: the Roman legions camping here, who managed to build a road right through it. There are remains of standing stones which show a much earlier occupation by the early Picts. Oliver Cromwell in 1651 camped his army here, as did the Duke of Buccleugh on his way with 10,000 men to fight the Covenanters at the Battle of Bothwell Bridge in 1678. Jacobite armies were here in 1715 and '45. Down the centuries, the famous residents of note have been fighters who have shown great heroism.

The name "Shotts" is actually taken from a resident here in the 1500s called Bartram de Shotts. A mythic character of a very violent nature, he was a giant of a man, standing over two metres tall, who was seen as a match for a dozen fighting men in battle. His reputation made the local sheriffs struggle to contain his raids on the unwary. Traders and travellers following the old Roman road would be attacked and robbed by this savage man, who would appear and slaughter them in lightning raids.

It got too much, with so many complaints that King James IV made an offer to whoever could capture or slay the giant: "a hawk's flight of land" to the brave fellow who undertook the task.

One who thought he could do it was the Laird of Muirhead. The Muirheads have had land in this area as far back as William the Lion in 1165. Our brave knight stalked the robber's movements in the area, and he carefully hunted down the giant Bartram de Shotts. Although he feared that he was no match at all in a straightforward one-to-one confrontation with Bartram, he knew that with cunning he could beat him! His plan was to hide, camouflaged in the undergrowth, close to a well he had observed the giant drinking from (called Kates Well).

Muirhead found a hiding place close to where Bartram de Shotts would stop and refresh himself. Once the giant was on his knees drinking from the well, Muirhead jumped out of hiding in the bushes and brought his broadsword down upon the giant's Achilles tendons on both legs, cutting them through, and rendering Bartram unable to rise and fight. The next blow from Muirhead's sword removed the giant's head. The head of Bartram de Shotts was presented to James IV, who was as good as his word and fulfilled his promise of a "hawk's flight's worth of land", which became Lauchope estate. The area where he killed the giant became "Shotts" after the giant who was slain there.

The Laird of Muirhead would not have long to enjoy the land he had secured for his family, as he was to fight at the ill-fated Battle of Flodden in 1513 and share the fate of the king who granted the "hawk's flight" charter of land.

They both, along with many thousands more, died in the action.

Whatever is in the water of the village of Shotts, it seems to create courage and heroism of a high degree. In fact, my reason for bringing Shotts to your attention in this book is not the tale of the brave Laird of Muirhead, although that on its own is an incredible story. Instead, let me tell you the heroic tale of Jamie Anderson.

Born to humble beginnings, Jamie Anderson would by good favour find himself the Master of Shotts in his manhood. A military man himself of the highest honour, his selfless actions in battle would help to turn a battle lost into Britain becoming the masters of Europe. Born in 1777, he was the second son of Sergeant-Major William Anderson.

Sergeant-Major Anderson led the 21st Regiment of North British Fusiliers during the American War of Independence. He himself was under command of Colonel James Inglis Hamilton.

After peace was settled with American independence, Sergeant-Major Anderson returned to Glasgow in a severely wounded condition, where his old commanding officer, not forgetting all his Sergeant-Major had done for him in America, provided what was necessary to give his young son Jamie a good education. Hamilton took on fatherly roles Jamie's own father was unable to perform due to his wounds.

Relations became so good, with Jamie's success at

school, that Colonel Hamilton encouraged him to take up a career in the army with the Dragoons.

Colonel James Inglis Hamilton took it upon himself to bestow every honour the young Jamie could achieve in his military education as an officer.

After his father's death in 1803 he was awarded the position of Cornet of the North British Dragoons. Because of this, Jamie Anderson changed his name to that of his benefactor Colonel James Inglis Hamilton. He became James Hamilton, and the old colonel made him his heir to Murdostoun Estate in Shotts, which included a castle. The colonel died in late 1803.

Jamie had an allowance of two hundred pounds in this position as well as his military pay. Over the next few years he impressed King George III who gave him the rank of Lieutenant-Colonel while giving his benefactor's regiment to him: the Scots Greys.

The Scots Greys were formed in 1678 and became the Royal Regiment of Scots Dragoons. A cavalry unit was formed from them in 1707, becoming the Royal Scots Dragoon Guards. They chose and bred only grey-coloured horses and took the nickname that stuck with the regiment – the "Scots Greys".

They saw action in battle at Killiecrankie in 1689 where they fought with General Mackay against Lord Dundee's Highlanders who had rebelled in an attempt to reinstate James VII on the throne. The Highlanders were 2,400 strong, and completely outnumbered, but they charged down a steep ravine to attack 4,000 heavily armed and waiting Redcoats. The Redcoats managed no more than three rounds of musket fire before the Highlanders were among them with claymore swords. At close range fighting the Highlanders turned the field into a massacre. Even though the Highlanders had lost a third of their force in the three point-blank volleys, it shows the worth of the broadsword that 1,500 Highlanders tore the 4,000 Redcoats to pieces, leaving over 2,000 dead. Mackay fought through to the high ground with the Scots Greys only to see his army stream off the field in total defeat. Although beaten, the Greys stood by their commander. They again saw action at the Battles of Schellenberg 1704, Blenheim 1704, Elixheim (Eliksem) 1705, Sherriffmuir 1715, and the Battle of Minden 1759.

On 18th of June 1815, the regiment of the Scots Greys, now under the command of Colonel James Hamilton, faced across a gully the armies of Emperor Napoleon of France in a field called Waterloo. The Greys were put in the third line at Waterloo, all 416 horses and men.

The Duke of Wellington had picked the ground well, the village of Waterloo would now give its name to one of the most vicious and bloody affairs of the 19th century. His army was 72,720 men strong, consisting of 36,273 British, 7,447 German and 21,000 Belgians. The rest of the troops were of inferior quality, marshalled into regiments with German officers called "the Brunswickers".

Facing the duke across the gentle sloping valley were Napoleon's veterans, all 74,000 of them displayed in their regiments, with 252 cannon. The two armies sat out an early morning downpour. Napoleon was very concerned about the mobility of his horse lancers and cannons in such wet conditions where the mud became fifteen centimetres deep. But it stopped and dried out for a few hours. By ten o'clock he ordered his left flank to attack the British on that wing. They were heavily protected by a farmhouse and its walls: the farm building of Hougoumont.

It was essential for Napoleon to rout the British as quickly as possible, because coming fast to the Duke of Wellington's assistance were 50,000 Prussians under Blücher, their old French-hating general, just 15 kilometres away, and marching fast.

If Napoleon could force the farmstead soldiers to retreat, he thought he could march his men forward, overlap the British centre and win the day. But although Wellington had positioned only 40,000 infantry before Napoleon and his cannon, he had placed many divisions of infantry and his cavalry over on the other side of the valley – hidden from view.

A cavalry charge, once committed to, could only continue its momentum for a while. With thousands in the charge, all it took was one horse to be shot dead and fall and dozens would have to try to navigate past the dead obstacle without suffering the same fate. Once the impetus of a charge was spent, horses were very vulnerable to infantry; a regroup and a further charge was what could create the most damage. But in the tightness of a three-kilometre battlefield and 140,000 men fighting in that space, it was obvious that any cavalry charge here could be a disaster. It would have been a massive gamble to commit the many thousands of best troops in what could be a massacre.

Hougoumont farm's defenders were still in action after three hours' fighting. The farm and its barns were on fire and the gates to the farm had been blown away by cannon. The French now pushed forward, with Napoleon's own brother Jérôme Bonaparte leading the assault. On the French side, 30,000 men had been committed to take the farm, but the defenders stood their ground and fought hard: many died, and others stood on the dead to take their place. The walls inside had dead men four deep in places. Fully 10,000 men had died in this action in over two hours of fighting – most wore the blue uniforms of France. But still the farm flew British colours.

By 1 p.m. there were reports of movement in the fields behind the French position a few miles distant. To Napoleon's horror, it was the vanguard of Blücher's troops arriving in their hundreds. It was obvious that the left wing was not going to break through in time to prevent the Prussians arriving. Now he had to gamble, and fast.

He sent the armies of his centre, 30,000 of them, to advance against Wellington's centre. The battle had to be won and time was against him!

The Grand Army advanced to the beat of the drum, a mass of cannons were ignited, firing overhead, hitting the British lines, bowling through stationary red uniforms and throwing limbs and bodies aside. At first the advancing French were clouded in smoke from their cannons, then through the smoke they came, shoulder to shoulder up the gentle slope towards the British lines to the slow beat of the drum! A glittering sea of frightening silver bayonets and dark blue uniforms with white leather straps. Officers were leading the way with sabres drawn. It was magnificent and frightening to watch this sea of steel, for the procedure of such trained and resolute men had won victories for France and Napoleon all over Europe for the last ten years.

At one hundred paces the French and British levelled muskets and there was a roar of fire and smoke; men screamed, and bodies by the hundred fell dead and injured as the lead shot flew. The accuracy of the French musketeers began to tell, and the British lines began to waver and fall. The Scottish highland regiments were in the thick of it, wearing colourful kilts and red jackets. But no bravery could withstand such fearful devastation. The red line of uniforms started to break and retreat. At this point the French sensed the day was theirs!

Wellington could see he was losing the battle, and ordered his cavalry, which was on the other side of the hill, to advance! This was the 1st Brigade: 1st and 2nd Life Guards, Royal Horse Guards, and Dragoon Guards, and the 2nd Brigade, called the Union Brigade as it consited of English, Scottish, and Irish regiments, including the Scots Greys. In all, 2,651 horses charged at the pressing French.

As they crested the hill into their own retreating infantry, the 92nd Gordon Highlanders shouted their battle cries, "Scotland forever!" and "Go at them the Greys!", and rejoined the fight. The cavalry hit the French infantry hard, blowing the forward ranks away. The Scots Greys hit the leading French infantry, the 45th, and captured their regiment's Eagle standard. Napoleon responded in kind, sending in three brigades of his own Cuirassier (wearing breast plate) and Chevau-léger (lancers).

Scotland Forever! by Lady Butler (1881) depicting the charge
of the Scots Greys at Waterloo.

This experienced cavalry crashed into the wave of
British horses, hitting side-on to the charge and stopping
the momentum, as in this terrible mêlée of noise and death,
many thousands fought it out in the tightest of spaces.
The Scots Greys, all 416 of them led by Colonel James
Hamilton, smashed through the French infantry and in a
chaotic frenzy of sabres took on the French lancers.

Fought to a standstill, the Greys had taken horrific
cannon and infantry fire in the charge. The lancers were
broken, but the Greys' brigade commander, Sir William
Ponsonby, was captured by the French lancers, then killed
when a party of the Greys tried to rescue him, and left
down on the field with many thousands of dead and dying.

Now James Hamilton fought on with his remaining
Greys. He took a sabre wound in the left arm from a French

horseman – his arm was severed and useless, but he took the horse's reins in his teeth and fought with his right arm, his cutlass inflicting wounds as he spurted his lifeblood away from his other useless arm.

He was seen fighting furiously. When this time his right arm was now severed by a French lancer, still the horse's reins were in his mouth and he had the French cannons now levelled directly at him at point blank range.

He was last seen by his men who followed his charge towards the cannons and destroyed the threat. Blood spurting from both stumps directing his charging horse with only his teeth, he shouted for the Greys to follow his charge on the guns. They did and destroyed the battery. The losses were horrendous. What the brave French gunners thought at the bloody spectacle of this screaming man – completely disabled and with his horse's reins in his mouth – galloping towards them leading the charge of what was left of the Scots Greys, can only be imagined. Some of the French gunners turned and ran, abandoning their guns on the field.

In this epic charge, the Scots Greys were nearly wiped out, and the other units of the Union Brigade suffered similar losses. Of the 2,651 cavalry that charged the French dragoons, 1,205 men and 1,303 horses never returned.

Colonel James Hamilton, laird of Murdostoun Castle in Shotts, was found in the morning, his body among the cannons he had led the charge against. Both arms were missing. But it had taken a bullet through the heart to stop the colonel.

The British cavalry charge with the Scots Greys has

been immortalised in many a painting – a screaming charge of colour and confusion. It was the turning point in the battle. Napoleon, seeing his forward lines smashed, sent in his reserve, the "Old Guard", experienced men who had seen dozens of victories under Napoleon. They marched to the beat of the drum up the hill to be shot to pieces by Wellington's men – divisions that he had held over the hill and safe from the cannonade. The whole French force collapsed as Blücher's men cut off their escape. Napoleon got away, leaving over 25,000 of his men dead on the field. The allies' loses were equally severe, around 20,000 men and 600 officers, including Colonel James Hamilton.

In Shotts, his wife would erect a memorial to her dead husband. It still stands today in Shotts churchyard. The castle and estate, with James Hamilton having no children, was passed on to Sir Alexander Ingles Cochrane, a younger son of Thomas the 8th Earl of Dundonald who was a distant relative of the old General Hamilton.

Never have I read of a braver man than Colonel Hamilton. He could have retired to seek a surgeon and possibly live to fight another day after he lost his arm…but no, he was made of sterner stuff and continued the charge on the enemy which cost him his life…as I said, the water in Shotts makes brave men!

Further reading

Bartram de Shotts…History of the Parish of Shotts, Grossart, 1880, p. 25/26

James Inglis Hamilton…History of the Parish of Shotts 1880, pp. 135-145

Waterloo...Great Battles of the British Army, 1869...
pp. 410-428

Waterloo...the War of Wars...Struggle between Britain
and France 1789-1815

Barbero...The Battle: A New History of Waterloo, 2005

Chapter 22

Hare Today! Gone Tomorrow

Edinburgh, the College of Surgeons, October 1828: the class today was going to be led by the esteemed Dr Knox, conducting the autopsy of a recently received cadaver. This on its own was a rare spectacle, as only hanged villains from the city were donated to the table of the surgeons for dissection before an open class.

Much was to be learned from the teachings of Dr Knox, but he was limited by the availability of his raw materials...criminals who had recently been hanged! And, although he was by law limited to one donated body per annum, the doctor had over recent months had quite a few classes...with a seemingly unlimited supply of bodies ready for dissection. Dr Knox's lessons were a must-see for the medical students in the school. This October in this class of Dr Knox, the students watching from the raised standing area above the dissection table were rather restless. The doctor's voice bellowed out with authority as he made his cuts. Stooping over the cadaver, he had his servant push back his spectacles every so often as he worked meticulously over the body. Usually he asked his students questions about the dissection, or identified certain hidden muscles and viscera, or answered eager questions, then continued the dissection.

Today was different: there was an uneasy silence and occasional mutterings from the crowd, till the doctor had

had enough and stopped to confront what was distracting him...."Well?" the doctor cried to his audience.

One stepped forward: "Sir, I feel we have a problem. That body there, I know the man. That's Jamie Wilson from the street, he's a beggar boy, an illiterate fool who entertains the street, he's afflicted by a club foot and has red hair. I would know him anywhere, as I saw him only two days past in good health. That, sir, is daft Jamie Wilson. I feel some mischief has befallen him to end here at this table."

This is the point at which the career of Dr Knox started to nose-dive to very great depths. A murder investigation began, exposing a system of merchandise that had been delivered into the good doctor's arms over the previous fifteen months...a cargo of death.

It must be said that grave robbing was nothing new, and it had become a constant terror for the newly bereaved. Many bodies had gone missing not long after burial and had found their way to autopsy studios in the lecture halls of medical students. The rate of one executed criminal a year was not enough for the studios that needed them, and so under-the-counter deals were done with very base characters to fetch more bodies for the classes. In many graveyards it had come to the point that armed guards had to stand in cemeteries to ward off the macabre practice.

The snatched bodies demanded by the medical associations were well paid for. Some prices were as high as £10 a cadaver (that was six months' wages for a teacher). I have found the historical example of Leven and Pittenweem parish – because of the threat of graverobbing

– going to the expense of putting armed sentries in their own graveyards for protection.

With Daft Jamie being positively identified, next came arrests of the graverobbers who had provided the raw materials to Knox. It was with some shock that officers raiding a house belonging to a Mr Burke found a female body stuffed under a bed – the next consignment due for delivery to Dr Knox! In time two men, William Burke and William Hare, were arrested and the story of a morbidly unacceptable career unfolded. It was found that they had produced at least seventeen bodies for the good doctor's table. They had started off digging up recent burials from Greyfriars old cemetery in Edinburgh. The method was to dig out one end of the coffin, smashing into it so they could place two hooks under the cadaver's arms, then pull it free of its coffin and out the grave. It did not take much to cover up the scene of the crime. And then they were off with a wheelbarrow to the surgeon's practice to receive their filthy lucre.

After being locked up in the jail, both men at first refused to talk, but when Hare was offered a pardon if he would confess to the crimes, he took the deal, exposing a career of graverobbing developing into murder.

His confession gave the names of: Joseph the Miller, Abigale Simpson, Mary Patterson, a woman named as Effie, Mrs Ostler, Anne Dougal, Elizabeth Haldane, Peggy Haldane, Majory Campbell Docherty, and James Wilson (daft Jamie). At least four others were pulled from anonymous graves.

With William Hare's acceptance of the pardon, he

confessed all, condemning his partner in crime to be hanged for all their murders together. They had both come over to Scotland from Ireland for work in digging out the Caledonian Canal, a major works putting a navigable route along the 97 kilometres between the Beauly Firth and Loch Linnhe.*

The two of them had settled in Edinburgh until they devised their next career turn. With the money earned from the canal digging, they bought a horse and cart which they loaded with cheaply bought crockery, and in which they acted like rag-and-bone men, collecting old iron in exchange for the crockery sets, and reselling it to iron smelters in Edinburgh.

After a chance meeting with Edinburgh College surgeon Dr Knox in an apothecary's shop (a chemist's), the deal was made to procure him bodies at £7.10s. a cadaver, rising to £10 for a fresh one. Quite a sum, considering a labourer made that in a year's pay.

With the acceptance of his pardon (known as turning King's Evidence) Hare was free to go! But as Burke dropped down through the hangman's trapdoor, a huge crowd in the thousands were still baying for Hare's death, outraged at the turn of events on their own doorstep.

Hare left the jail at nightfall and slipped into the shadows. He led his life in numerous small villages, but as

---

* It is interesting to note here that this construction was one of the Brahan Seer's predictions, (see the chapter "The Brahan Seer" in this book!). He predicted that full sailed ships would progress around Tomnahuric near Inverness in his predictions of 1620, made before his awful burning and death, a full two centuries before it actually happened.

soon as he was recognised, he was chased out by angry mobs.

It is on record that he managed to set up a toffee making business in Fife on the borders of Leven and Largo Parish in some bothy hidden away in the trees of Silverburn forest. He did manage to exist here for a period, but the rumour spread among children, his main clientele, that a child's finger had been found embedded in the toffee he sold. Not long after this, he was on the run again, pursued wherever he went by unruly mobs bent on his destruction.

His miserable life was to take him back home to Northern Ireland under a different guise and name. It was not until May in 1841 that two Irish labourers found a distressed man on the turnpike road in the parish of Orrey in County Tyrone. This was the Barony of Kilmore. They carried the man who called himself William McGuigan. He was in a sorry state but guided the helpful lads to bring him to where he had been staying, in the obscure village of Orrey.

They laid the man down in his miserable hut. Living in a loathsome poverty-stricken abode, with the coarsest of fare, his conditions had brought on a diseased existence for the man. It was obvious that he was dying. A priest was brought, and the most amazing confession started, that frightened the residents of Orrey into thinking that the Devil himself had been living among them for several years totally unknown. A guilty conscience and a deeply haunted troubled mind exposed the shocking truth.

His real name was William Hare. Finally, after being

chased out of every village he sought to live in, he had made it back home to Northern Ireland where in obscurity he had lived his final years, keeping away from company lest they uncover the truth about him. A false name had done him well but his life had been dragged out in terrible poverty. In his dreams, his old friend and business partner William Burke was there, taunting him with the noose around his neck. As he fell into a troubled sleep in front of his priest and others, he would arch his back in pain "like a thousand furies were on him". He cried out: "Burke! Burke! The scaffold, I see it, I see it!" Then he would settle again in the discomfort of a heavily troubled mind.

He told of his upbringing in Ireland, petty crimes turning to burglary. And in Scotland from an honest living at first, he had turned to grave robbing and finally murder. He continued talking to his priest till finally at two in the morning he passed away. The confession had made him tranquil, and it seemed a great relief to finally tell his story. An immense crowd had gathered by morning as gossip spread of the famous – or notorious – visitor who had just died. The police took possession of the body, and later he was buried in the grounds of Kilkeel Workhouse. It was a workhouse for women – those who had had children outside marriage and those who were unemployed. It housed three hundred inmates. Hare was buried in an unmarked grave as privately as possible.

His story was published in the penny broadsheet newspapers, printed by G. Whitelaw. It was recounted that he died on Saturday 29th May, 1841 in the Parish of Orrey/

Kilmore in County Tyrone...his death was witnessed by Captain Murray, a prominent figure in the town.

When Burke was hanged his body was laid out in the Surgeons' Hall of the College, to be viewed by the public before his own dissection. Over 24,000 people went through the room to view the dead man. Dr Knox was ruined by the scandal and had to leave his practice in Edinburgh. Because of Burke and Hare's bodysnatching to Dr Knox's orders, the Anatomy Act or "Warburton Act" was issued from Parliament in 1832, which allowed donated bodies to be used in surgeons' colleges. This would allow more bodies for dissection, and with plentiful donations it would ruin the trade of would-be body snatchers. Today Burke's skeleton still stands on display in the Anatomy Museum of Edinburgh University; he was only 1.65 metres tall. And a book was bound in the tanned skin of William Burke.

A further interesting footnote to this story...

In 1851 at the Glasgow Circuit court, Archibald Hare, aged 27, was found guilty of the murder of a man by stabbing him in the town of Blantyre. The newspapers described him as "repulsive and dogged". He was found guilty and hanged on the 24th October. His hanging was a mess: when he dropped through the trapdoor, he only fell two feet and the rope spun out of control as the body leapt about fighting for life. Murdoch the hangman had to jump down from the scaffold and hold on to Archibald's legs and pull, swinging like a pendulum till Archibald was strangled. Archibald Hare was the nephew of William Hare...murder, it seems, ran in the family!

Further reading

Burke's Hanging...The Scots Black Kalendar, p. 38-40

Archibald Hare...The Scots Black Kalendar, p. 58

William Hare...Living Largo

Parish borders...Bygone Fife...James Wilkie, p. 151

William Hare... death/confession... Broadsheet newspaper...printer G Whitelaw.

Chapter 23

For Sale, a Mackintosh

Throughout history harsh laws have been in force in Scotland to restrict women to being no more than childbearing house labourers. From the Parish Registers of St Andrews 1597 it declares in Law...

> concludit and ordeinit that na elder nor diacun suffir ane singill woman, that never hes bein mareit, to dwell hir allane in ane hous undelaited to the sessioune of the kirk, under the pain of vjs. viijd. first fault and xs. for the secund fault.
>
> (Concluding and ordained that no elder or Deacon suffer a single woman, never married, to dwell all alone in a house without permission from the parish under pain of 6 shillings 8 pence for first crime and 10 shillings for second)

Under this parish by-law, women lived on their own in great peril, for the church was always watching for signs of what were termed "orray women". To be caught in fornication three times would result in banishment from a town, which on its own could be an effective death sentence. Hoping another parish would welcome you within its borders as a waif and homeless stray was optimistic.

A girl could be married at twelve years of age. In the kirk register again, the St Andrews Register, a Robert Alexander (14) and Agnes Wishart from Mountflovry

(Mountflourie Leven) are preparing to get married with the blessing of the parish. In the First Book of Discipline, written by John Knox and others in 1560, it states…

> Mariage ought not to be contracted amongst persons, that have no election for lack of understanding. And therefore we affirme that bairns and infants cannot lawfully be married in their minor age, to wit, the man within 14 yeares, and the woman 12 yeares at least.

In 1496 the Scottish Education Act ordained…

> Item, it is statute and ordanit throw all the realme that all barronis and frehaldaris that ar of substance put thair eldest sonnis and airis to the sculis fra thai be aucht or nyne geiris of age and till remane at the grammer Sculis quhill thai be competentlie foundit and have perfite Latyne, and thaireftir to remane thre yeris at the sculis of art and jure, sua that thai may have knawlege and understanding of the lawis.
>
> (It is now law through out the realm that all Barons and Freeholders that are of substance put their eldest sons and heirs to the schools from 8 or 9 years of age and remain at grammar school till they have perfect latin and to remain for 3 years at the school of art and jury to have knowledge and understanding of the laws.)

Back in the fifteenth century, no education whatsoever was intended for women. But by 1828, which is the date of our next story, sewing schools at least had opened up for girls in Edinburgh. Overall literacy among women was still poor.

By the rules of marriage, a woman became her husband's property. A married woman had few if any rights, and certainly they had none concerning property and they could not make a will without their husband's permission. Men also had considerable flexibility in disciplining a woman – she could legally be beaten – and the criminal courts refused to recognise woman as witnesses. Responsibility for a woman's actions would be passed to her husband.

All in all a woman's lot was not so happy…she could not sell property, sue in court or make any business contracts without the husband's permission. In the Pittenweem burgh court in 1663 Christian Duncan had to agree to stop "scolding and calumniating her husband" (and also a woman he had been consorting with). Her punishment if she persisted in shouting at her husband would be to be publicly put in the 'jougs' – a metal collar and chain used like the stocks – and also to suffer a sound whipping, as well as any additional punishment the bailies thought appropriate!

Before 1891, women were very rarely allowed to divorce. Most women worked in a trade from an early age – as young as eight years old. With this as the background, I bring you the tale of Mary Mackintosh.

Nothing much is noted of Mary Mackintosh's life before the evening of Wednesday 16th July, 1828, but that afternoon her husband Thomas McGuisgan told her they were going to the Edinburgh's famous Grassmarket. As they approached the market he pulled out a placard, put it round her neck and led her into the livestock auctioneers' ring, dragging her with a rope made of straw. Her sign read…"To be sold by public auction!"

The auctioneer was a knight of the hammer, a pensioner with the name John F—n. He started business like he would with any farm beast. A Highland drover came forward. His beasts having been delivered to market and sold, he took an interest in the sale – he offered the first bid, saying, "She be a good like lassie, I will gie ten and twenty shillings for her!"

A great shout came from the crowd. Then another man declared she shouldn't go into the Highlands, and bid sixpence more for her.

A great crowd had gathered, and people were coming out the taverns to see the action. One of the Irish pig farmers from Killarney was totally drunk, but joined in the fun: "I will give two shillings more, for she is a pretty woman."

Now another drunk came came out of the tavern (a shoemaker from Newry) and hit the pig farmer ("in the bread bag"). He was out of action for ten minutes, making the woman for sale laugh heartily, while the crowd cheered in support. The shoemaker went to the auctioneer to make it known there were now three live bids for the woman on the table. But he knocked the auctioneer over in his inebriation. This brought a great cheer again for the entertainment of the crowd.

But word had got around of the ludicrous sale, the women of the neighbourhood spread the gossip faster than a champion sprinter running a hundred metres! They gathered to the number of seven hundred. Edinburgh has seen its fair share of fighting over the years, against Romans, Saxons, Angles and the English, but never had it experienced the wrath of its own womanhood. They came in vengeance for their sex; they came with years of pent-up anger and repression; they came with a fury that if it could only be harnessed would power a rocket to the moon!

They had armed themselves by putting stones in freshly knitted socks. Then they charged, swinging the sock weapons in the air…and this wave of unstoppable feminine fury assaulted the mob in a vicious charge, knocking the men down like skittles!

They never stood a chance. The men fell and dispersed quickly before a tide of aggressive womanhood, leaving the wounded behind unable to defend themselves against this violent female mob. The poor auctioneer barely got away with his life, attacked with the stone-swinging socks he got away with bruising. They "scratched and tore his face in a dreadful manner."

But Thomas McGuisgan did not want to lose his sale, and so – foolishly – he stood his ground…until a swinging sock found its mark, and he was knocked unconscious. The woman who smote the mighty blow was a sweep's wife who, it is said, displayed great bravery in support of her sex. She screamed at the fallen husband, "I will learn you to auction your wife again, you contaminated villain."

Coming back to his senses, Thomas hit her between

her eyes with a swift punch, which was followed by the woman's chimney-sweep husband getting stuck in, and there was a great mêlée of violence. The multitude of women sallied forth unleashing their weapons and beat Thomas to the floor. A great battle now ensued, with the remaining bemused men standing laughing at the spectacle.

The town's police now arrived and saved the men from a sound beating…maybe even deaths! The poor beaten and scratched auctioneer screamed above the din that as he could not be protected, he would have no more business with the sale. But order was restored, and the auction started again: a new bidder offered five shillings above the last price. A handsome farmer and a friend of Mary Mackintosh, he bid again. Two pounds five shillings, and the auctioneer, desperate to finish, declared her sold!

The farmer had won her. He beckoned her to him, to climb up on his horse. She was pulled up, and the woman wrapped her arms around the man and seemed happy. The crowd roared at her in support and Mary rode off into the distance with her man in shining armour.

Today we would know nothing of this story had it not been written about in a broadsheet newspaper in 1828. The broadsheets were popular single-sheet papers sold on street corners for a penny. The National Library of Scotland holds 25,000 examples, of which no 1268 is the story of Mary Mackintosh's sale.

Further reading

Marriage laws...Ewan...The Early Modern family, p. 273, 275

St Andrews Kirk session register...1582-1600...orray women, p. 836

1486 Scottish Education Act, p. 56...St Andrews parish sessions, vol 1

Chapter 24

The Kirkcaldy Parish Disaster

Back in 1990, I had been living in London for three years. I was spoilt with live concerts, The Stranglers one night, Blondie the next – there was that quality of live music every week. But one night saw me at Earls Court in London...and Pink Floyd doing their new album "The Division Bell". Earls Court stadium was a new venue for me: its broad expanse and good view for the audience were to my liking. I had tickets for seats with a clear view of the stage, albeit near the back rows. A packed audience of near 16,000 went quiet as the music hummed and gathered pace. Slowly the band members were lit up in lights as the noise gathered and the audience roared into life with the band's opening number, "Shine on you crazy diamond". The floor vibrated around me, suddenly the seats rose gently. All around me were faces full of bewilderment as the seating continued to rise. Then I looked over my shoulder and the screaming started.

The seating behind me for, say, twenty rows, had collapsed. Bodies and chairs intermingled in the chaos. The band on stage, realising something dramatic had happened in the audience, stopped the concert. The concert security was quickly on the scene and people were gently helped to safety. The panic was minimal, it was quite orderly and those who were hurt were gently pulled away to be treated. The whole elevated seating complex had collapsed in on itself. But luckily only a few broken legs as far as I remember. The gig was rescheduled and because I was in the area that collapsed, I got a free tour tee-shirt with "survivor of Earls Court" on it. I felt very privileged, and to add to my joy, Pink Floyd when they replayed at Earls Court was my all-time number three top concert, out of the hundreds I have been too...after The Sex Pistols at Brixton Academy and Simple Minds at Wembley.

Our next story has similarities to the Earls Court accident. It was heavy numbers of people that caused the following chaos, leaving 35 dead and about double that number injured. But this time it wasn't a concert that attracted the big numbers of people, it was a communion in a church, in Kirkcaldy, Fife, in 1828.

It's a fact that today's church in Scotland is failing. Audiences in some parishes are down to single figures as members of the congregation find other worthwhile things to do with their Sunday instead of listening to a minister with his large wage and large house telling them God is good!

But back in the early 19th century a normal Sunday would have your family dressed in their best clothes and attending church service at 11am, then home for dinner, followed by church service again at 2.30pm, then 5pm Sunday school...followed by an evening service. That's church four times on a Sunday! It is obvious that, unlike today, the church in early 19th-century Scotland was very important for the Fife people.

And this is where we find ourselves, in Fife, the town of Kirkcaldy: at the parish kirk on Sunday, June 15th for the 6pm evening communion service. There was a bit of excitement as the guest speaker was Reverend Edward Irving from the Caledonian Church in London. He was the son-in-law of the current minister, and a former Kirkcaldy resident.

The church bells were ringing, and the parishioners were coming, producing a healthy congregation. The ground floor filled up fast and the balcony section had almost reached its 250-seat maximum. The bells continued to toll for another ten minutes as the stragglers hurried in and the doors were bolted. A quiet went around the packed house as, through the vestry, the guest speaker could be seen getting prepared to walk out to commence the awaited service. It was Mr Edward Sang, who was sitting underneath the balcony, right under the thick longitudinal beam supporting the upper level, who saw the danger first.

First there was a small quantity of dust that fell – it had particles of lime. He looked up and observed the whole mass of the floor above coming down, as it were, in a body. He made a desperate spring forward into the vestry leading to the pulpit. By the time he landed at this spot the whole upper area had collapsed in on the people standing in the galley below! It had held 250 seats plus the untold numbers standing at the back. All of the above had fallen onto the people below.

He observed a small boy about eight years old make a similar escape before the lot came down, but his mother was crushed lifeless against the back wall where they had stood. She was still holding on to his hand, even in death. One individual had his whole family with him. Standing in the centre of the downstairs area Gallery he gathered his family in his arms and remained still with them, as more debris fell and screams, and pandemonium reigned around him.

The crowd that untangled themselves from the fallen timber and chaos fought their way en masse to the locked doors of the parish kirk, where hundreds now in full panic were fighting to escape death. A man of great height and strength pushed his way to the front of the screaming mob and with difficulty unlatched the door. They sprawled outwards, pouring themselves in a heap of misery and panic into the concrete pathway. The old and young fell in heaps, trampled by their companions in the sea of hundreds of bodies fighting to escape. The man who had fought his way to open the locked doors, later found his daughter had succumbed to the stampede – killed by the very persons he had helped escape.

One woman called Sarah Penman was peculiarly unfortunate, losing her husband and son in the collapse and herself being so trampled in the crush to escape that her body could only be identified by the colour of her gown. Another woman killed in the stampede, showed no sign of injury except one hobnailed shoe print on her chest. That alone had caved her ribs in, causing her death.

Once the church was emptied and the disaster could be seen for what it was…the butcher's bill was atrocious. Twenty-eight local people dead and positively identified, with another seven bodies so mangled in the stampede to get out, they simply could not be identified because of their injuries. Many of the injured were women who were pulled unconscious from the debris and later had no recollection of what had happened.

A local architect surveyed the resulting damage and reached some shocking conclusions about the accident. From the remains of the south galley area, he was astonished to see that some of the joists of the great beam had no supports to prevent their fall other than the nails that attached them to the floor. Further, he observed that the pillars which supported the beams of the north galley were not placed in the centre but towards the outer angle, possibly to avoid congregation having a substantial pillar of wood blocking their view of the pulpit.

The dead that they could identify were named as...

Agness Smith...a mill spinner,

Martha Mathewson...28 years old...mill spinner,

Jean Mathewson...24 years old...mill spinner,

Issoble Mathewson...22 years old...mill spinner,

Mrs Beverage,

Grace Cunningham,

Mary Anderson...16 years old,

Thomas Miller...13 years old,

Janet Cunningham...13-year-old servant,

Peter Nicol...8 years old,

Janet Currer...servant,

Henrietta Brown...spinster,

Nancy Johnstone...lived at Pathhead,

Janet Stenhouse...from Westbridge,

Wemyss Murray...from Newtown Abbots hall,

Mrs Watson...from Kirkcaldy,

Sarah Penman...a poultry keeper in Dunniker,

Elizabeth Irvine...servant at Glentarkie,

David Lawson...weaver at Kirkcaldy,

Robert McCaul...19 years old,

John Hepburn...shoe maker,

John Barron ...flax dresser,

John Brown...weaver from Pathhead,

Alex Mc Dougall...from Kinghorn,

James Oswald...father in law to the above,

Miss Wingate...from Glasgow,

Mathew Brodie...a Kirkcaldy weaver,

Jas Grant...tailor...died the following Tuesday from his injuries.

Seven more bodies made up the number of dead to 35. They could not be identified, their faces were so damaged by the disaster. By the following weekend the mounds of twenty graves were present in the church yard formed in a rough hillock, where a week before there was none!

The church today is still functioning as a community resource. I was invited to lecture here by the Kirkcaldy Civic Society about my book *The Weem Witch* in 2014. The inside is indeed huge, the stage and amenities first-class for a lecture. There were no balconies as I remember. And at the time I was unaware of the hellish accident that had happened in this lovely location.

Further reading

CHEAP TRACTS, pamphlet no 8...An account of the dreadful accident and loss of life which occurred in

Kirkcaldy, June 15, 1828 (printed by John Miller, Dunfermline, 1828)

Scottish church life...Recollections of EAST FIFE FISHER FOLK...Belle Patrick, 2003

Chapter 25

Mr McLeod's Dream Evidence

The parish of Assynt sits in the north-westerly area of Scotland, a wild, rugged, windswept, glacier-moulded, mountainous landscape. In this area of 480 square kilometres, the deer are more numerous than humans. Today only six hundred people live in Assynt, existing on sheep farming and crofting, a lonesome lifestyle characterised by hairy jerseys and hardiness. Back in 1830, the highland clearances had destroyed this region, sheep farming replacing the clan's people. In 1830 the population was barely 100 souls. Into this location walked Murdoch Grant, a pedlar making his way from croft to croft earning a squalid but comfortable living with his horse in tow.

Murdoch appreciated the summer sun's heat as he trekked along the dirt-track road towards his next customer in the next glen. Midges were his biggest hazard in June: the tiny mosquito-like Scottish insect with jaws like a shark was an ever-present pest. (The author can vouch for this: I was nearly eaten to death in this location.) Along the high mountains the eagles cried in the sky, the solitude was broken by a figure in the distance...a man waving as he picked up pace to reach him. Murdoch steadied his horse and reached under the saddle for a small half-bottle of whisky to offer his guest.

He sat back on a rock as the man approached. "Hi friend, what ails ye?" he called, offering the bottle. The man, out of breath, took the bottle, smiled, raised it to salute the offer of it, had a drink and returned it, whereupon Murdoch himself tasted it and then turned to return it to the pouch under the saddle. With his back to his guest, his bottle was the last thing he would ever see…his skull was smashed with a heavy cosh!

Murdoch's body would be found floating in one of the mountain pools four weeks later. When pulled from the waters in what seemed like a tragic accident, his pockets were found to be pulled out and his purse was missing. From these circumstances an act of foul play was deduced.

At Inverness, the authorities who were investigating the crime suddenly found a local teacher, Hugh Macleod, very enthusiastic in helping the police. He said he knew the man, was most helpful in descriptions, and said he knew the pathways in Assynt where Murdoch Grant walked towards his customers. It was through Hugh's help that they were able to piece together Murdoch's route and fathom out where the villainy took place.

Then it was brought to the attention of the sheriff of Inverness that Hugh Macleod had actually changed a ten pound note for smaller amounts at the local post office not long before. Ten pounds was a lot of money then, and when he was detained Macleod had no satisfactory explanation for how he had come by such a large sum. It was suspected that Hugh's willingness to help might be hiding some other secret, but without more evidence the sheriff would eventually have to release him.

The Highlands have always been renowned for their poets and storytellers, with very little actually being written down and preserved. Much of the folklore and legends have been told around fireplaces in a tradition of word-of-mouth preservation. Highland "seers" were common, some being utterly remarkable in their predictions, such as the Brahan Seer as described in Chapter 9. In 1831 one of these remarkable men stepped forward in Inverness, after they had kept Hugh Macleod in jail for nearly a year while they sought evidence to convict him.

Kenneth Fraser, a local tailor, came forward to the sheriff with an amazing piece of the murder puzzle. Kenneth claimed to see things in his own dreams, and in this instance, he had seen the pedlar's backpack, the one he always travelled with, the one he had been carrying when murdered from behind. He had viewed it in his dream hidden under a cairn of rocks: in his vision, he had seen Hugh Macleod build the cairn. It was not to be found in the immediate area where Murdoch's body was pulled from the cold loch, but further west.

A search was called for and indeed in the exact area predicted by the seer Kenneth Fraser, a heap of rocks was found piled up in a rough cairn. Once it was opened, there was the pedlar's backpack holding his clothes and meagre possessions.

A trial was set for 26th September with Lords Moncreiff and Medwyn sitting as judges. All day and night the trial lasted, as the proceedings were enacted in front of the jury. When it came to their turn the jury took a mere fifteen minutes to find Hugh Macleod...guilty!

Hugh Macleod professed astonishment at the verdict and shouted, "The Lord almighty knows that I am innocent! I did not fathom anyone in this country could be condemned on mere opinion." The sentence of death was passed on Hugh…to be carried out on 24 October.

He was taken back to the Inverness Tolbooth jail to await the erection of the gallows in an area called the Longman to the north of the town. It was then, sitting in the small jail cell, that Hugh's conscience got the better of him: he completely confessed to his actions in the murder, and awaited his fate!

He was collected from the jail and led along wearing a long black cape with a white cap on his head. A rope was placed around his neck and the hangman pulled him along the road with the townspeople of Inverness shouting their disgust at the condemned man. Hugh was carrying a huge bible, and he sang some psalms which were then taken up by the crowd as he passed along the road to the gallows. At the scaffold a religious service was held, and Hugh now addressed the crowd in Gaelic offering his remorse for his actions. His signal of a dropped handkerchief was for the hangman to draw the bolt that would spring the trapdoor open so that Hugh could fall six feet to his doom! His body was left hanging for three quarters of an hour, then cut down and sent to Edinburgh College of Surgeons where it was to be dissected, as were all criminal cases.

Chapter 26

The Loch Fyne Quarry Disaster

In Glasgow, September 1886, An advertisement in the *Telegraph* newspaper announced that another "monster blast" was to be undertaken at the Crarae stone quarry on the banks of Loch Fyne. Special bookings were being offered to the public figures of Glasgow for a ride in the luxurious paddle steamer *Lord of the Isles*, and it was planned to anchor the boat a few hundred yards from the quarry and – with a champagne lunch – witness the explosion.

It was set for one o'clock on the 25th September. The blast was to begin after a signal whistle from the ferry boat, then the celebrations could start.

The explosion was going to be mightily impressive, with a massive seven tonnes of gunpowder to be used in the forthcoming blast. The explosion was estimated to release 90,000 tonnes of rock face. For over thirty years, such rock had been mined for use on the City of Glasgow's pavements by the Sim Company, owned by William Sim. The cut slabs were shipped down Loch Fyne to Greenock docks and transported to Glasgow. The company had a unblemished safety record and proudly boasted not one fatality since opening in 1852. It was seen by Glasgow's Labour council chiefs as a great moment to celebrate their own Jubilee and therefore they took full control of the expedition.

The steamer would sail from Greenock bound for

Kirn Dunoon, the Kyles of Bute and Loch Fyne, finishing at Inveraray then returning straight to Greenock. The event certainly caught the imagination of Glasgow's upper-crust citizens, over one thousand passengers were booked on board the paddle steamer, *Lord of the Isles*. It was planned that with a signal from the ferry, the engineers of the mine would set off the explosion, with the ferry passengers getting a spectacular view, not two hundred metres away from the quarry.

The charges for the blast had been bored into the stone face 10 metres above the water line. They extended 20 metres horizontally with chambers dug every 7 metres to place the charges in. The cavities had been set and filled with gunpowder.

All one thousand passengers stood on deck as the minutes passed to detonation time. The ferry gently slowed as it came up the loch and was soon in view of the quarry. As it sounded its whistle to make itself known, a great cheer went from the paying guests. On land the employees of the mine made final preparations, testing electric wires that would ignite the charge. It was ten minutes to one. On board the ferry the passengers were dressed in their finery, bow ties and top hats. This was a prestige trip, with some of Glasgow's finest turning out for the spectacular event. Most were guests of the City Council and every space was taken as they jostled on deck for the best view.

The time ticked closer to the one o'clock deadline, and a hush descended on board. Suddenly there was the shrill shriek of the ferry's steam whistle. Three seconds later it was answered by the cascading rumble of a vast explosion.

The huge rockface fell in a sheet, the smoke and debris rose in the air like a mushroom plume! And as if the blast was a signal, heavy rain now fell from the darkened skies. The audience roared and clapped their appreciation of the fantastic blast: a success all round as drinks were raised and general merriment continued. The ferry captain wanted to turn the boat around and continue its planned voyage up Loch Fyne. But a portion of the passengers wanted a closer view of the mine and the chance of a small rock souvenir. Two hundred passengers decided to disembark from the ferry, walk the short distance to view the quarry and stay an hour or so as the boat sped on up Loch Fyne.

With the Glasgow Labour council chiefs leading the way, the land party waited for the dust to settle, then marched to the Crarae Mine gateway. The rain was falling and darkened skies promised even more unpleasantness but that did not dishearten the souvenir collectors as they walked through the gates. High up on the hillside an engineer, with his facemask raised, shouted down to the crowd, but his words could not be distinguished clearly through the falling rain.

First to fall was Labour councillor John Young, in top hat and dinner jacket, fit for a ballroom. He collapsed suddenly, soiling his fine clothes with the dust and filth of the rock fall. Fellow councillor Thomas Duncan leaned to give a hand to his fallen companion, then he himself sank to his knees, and fell as prostrate as his friend. Then fell Matthew Waddell, a Glasgow restaurant owner, and Mathew Steel, a jeweller. Peter Stevenson and James Shaw fell with a wave of others. John Small also went down as invisible death overtook them! Another seventy people were affected.

Panic now ensued from the other passengers as they fought to escape back through the gateway. Women screamed, as men pulled unconscious comrades away from the mass of felled bodies before they too were overcome.

After an hour the ferry returned, to a scene of panic and pandemonium.

The mine, needing relatively flat slabs for its paving work on the Glasgow streets, preferred gunpowder to the usual high explosive dynamite. Dynamite shattered the rock into pieces and was too destructive.

Gunpowder, if used properly, could leave the rocks in sheet form. The mine used seven tonnes of the powder, which when set off would release toxic gases including carbonic monoxide, carbon dioxide, and sulphur dioxide. In sufficient concentrations, these mixtures cause immediate asphyxiation if breathed in. Obviously, the engineer's shouted warning could not be heard by the party. The mine needed a good time to clear its poisonous fumes, and the eagerness of the Labour councillors to survey their entertainment brought calamity amongst their party. The heavy rain had stopped the usual dispersal of the fumes: as the party walked to the face of the mine...death was waiting for them!

There were seven dead and fifty others hospitalised with lung damage: a total disaster on a day of joviality turned to terror.

The *Telegraph* newspaper reported the disaster as:

The 405-tonne luxury paddle steamer transported the bodies of the fallen and injured to Glasgow. *Lord of the Isles* was soon to be taken off this route and directed to work in London. Built on the Clyde by D W Henderson in 1877 for the Inveraray Steam Boat Company, she had been in service in Scotland for thirteen years. On the Thames she suffered terrible damage when both funnels were smashed off while navigating under London Bridge. A foolish captain had misjudged the height. She was sold and renamed the *Jupiter*, running from Southgate to Margate, but was sold back to the Clyde boat masters in 1904 and she worked for a year as *Lady of the Isles* …she was scrapped at Dumbarton docks in 1905.

Recently the author took a ferry to Mull from Oban, to take some photographs…the name of my ferry?…*Lord of the Isles*.

I'm in great debt to the fantastic Quarry View Coffee Shop at Crarae Minard, Argyll, sitting straight across from the mine itself. They still have the newspaper cuttings from the *Telegraph* and several letters of condolence in a glass frame in the café…without which, apart from enjoying a great breakfast here, I would know nothing of this story.

For information on the gases created by gunpowder my thanks to Clarice Wilson (criminal forensic scientist) and Michael Simpson ex-army.

THE ILLUSTRATED LONDON NEWS.

No. 2477.—VOL. LXXXIX.　　SATURDAY, OCTOBER 9, 1886.　　WITH EXTRA SUPPLEMENT | SIXPENCE

THE DISASTER IN SCOTLAND: SUFFOCATION BY GAS FROM GUNPOWDER BLASTING.

Newspaper illustrations of the quarry disaster.

Chapter 27

Jack the Ripper...in Pittenweem

It is October 1888. The sea fog swirls thick across the streets of the fishing village of Pittenween, blocking out the street lamps, and reducing them to a rancid glow. There is no wind, the silence is broken only by the clinking of the moored boats' rigging, gently swaying in the harbour with the rising tide. The hour is late, some piano playing can be heard, the two inns on the sea front have done the usual business, drunken sea hands are making their way homeward, and here and there ladies of the night mingle with men who still have some coin to spend. In the shadows steps one who has a deadly purpose. He wants to deal in one business tonight...death...the name he is known by...Jack the Ripper.

In 1888 a bloodthirsty fiend had been stalking the lowborn products of the Whitechapel area in the East End of London. Brutally slaying a number of prostitutes, he taunted the police in letters, with severed bits of cadavers sent as proof...all this from a man who signed himself...Jack the Ripper!

He teased the authorities with phrases in his letters such as "Catch me if you can", and by 1st October he had brutally murdered four young women. The police had made his first "Jack the Ripper" letter public, and the newspapers went into a frenzy about the possible identity of the man responsible...But five hundred miles from

Whitechapel, at Cornceres in the Fife fishing village of Kilrenny, farmer David Edie had just opened his mail. The threatening letter he had received was signed off with …

"I remain yours truly…JACK THE RIPPER."

His letter read…

> Dear Sir,
>
> As I was walking down the road today I saw your two sons and O! O! the pride in them is something awful. The boy who told me that had corderoys on, and he told me that Charles, the second boy, was the pridefulest boy in the school, and that he was in his class. I think I heard that some boys called him Andrew. We passed some boys and never looked at them, so I have been employed by one who hates you very much to kill you all, which I will soon do, for I will not come to Anstruther for nothing. After I am done with you all, I will murder in Anster and Pittenweem here, so be on your guard, for I will murder you all before the year is gone, so that will put down pride. What is pride? Pride is self-conceit, so I will do what I have done in Whitechapel. The last day you have on earth is the 21st November, at half-past eleven at night. Another person I am informed about was Jamieson, but I will write to him too, soon.
>
> I remain, yours truly,
> JACK THE RIPPER

According to its postmark, this frightening letter had been posted in Pittenweem. The date on the postmark was

October 15th. It was evident that whoever was calling himself "Jack the Ripper" had posted a letter there…he was in Pittenweem!

Another letter was addressed to the Reverend Andrew Douglas, the minister of Abbey Parish in Arbroath. Recently, on the 10th September, the still of the night at his home in Arbroath had been severely disturbed by a gunshot shattering his study window as he worked. The mystery deepened as he received the first of his threatening letters…it again, like farmer David Edie's letter, promised death to him and his family, signing off as "your assassin".

Next came letters to the local newspapers. One was sent to Mr Russel, the editor of the *East of Fife Record* making more threats and uncannily signing off with the same rhetoric that the Whitechapel Ripper had recently offered to the London newspapers…"CATCH ME IF YOU CAN".

The letters kept coming to Mr Russel and David Edie, always with threats and promising murder. One took credit for the recent death of a young boy in Pittenweem called Alexander Robinson. Aged only four, he was last seen alive on 1st October 1888. He had been caught by a wave and carried away…his body was never found!

The mystery hate mailer admitted he "was the murderer" and called for the last letter to be inserted into the *East of Fife Record* newspaper and made public. The Reverend Mr Douglas received his latest letter. It read…

> Sir,
> Although I am just now staying here I am waiting for a chance for your life, which I hope will

soon be taken. You have done me very much harm, so you will suffer for it. Don't think you will get away with it – no, no. Watch at night, for some night the bloody deed will be perpetrated. I will not shoot you this time, but will murder you. I have plenty more who are willing to do it. I will scatter your brains through your house, but will not touch your wife. So enjoy yourself for a while. Then you will be no more.

Goodbye. Rev Mr Douglas

This letter had a postmark from Anstruther, another Fife village. It had been sent on 26th September 1888.

Enter Inspector Maiden, of St Andrews police. He now had the job of finding the threatening letter sender who signed himself "Jack the Ripper". Maiden had to hand the latest three letters sent to the three victims. He took his search close to the locations where the letters had been posted, and thinking the culprit might be a schoolboy, he visited the school of Waid Academy in Anstruther, half a mile from the town of Pittenweem. His plan was to review the papers written by the boys at the school, to see if he could possibly get a match in the handwriting. After an age of searching hundreds of exercise books, he came across what he considered was a good match.

"I was of the opinion that the handwriting of the works when compared with the School books, the handwriting corresponded with one of the textbooks."

Robert Jackson, the head teacher, agreed with the match between the school jotters and the letters. After this, the evidence was taken to an expert in Edinburgh, lithograph writer James Melville. He was struck by the similarities of the capital letters "A" and "I", and found that words such as "kill" and "murder" and also "pride" were identical across the letters and school notebooks.

It was his clear expert opinion that the writing belonged to John Peter Watson, who was a schoolboy at Waid Academy. This boy lived in Pittenweem, and was thirteen years old!

The arrest was made. Proceedings took place in the sheriff court in Cupar. On the 3rd November, John Peter Watson, with his mother and father in the space at the bar reserved for counsel, heard the charges made against him...and denied them!

The boy was charged with having written a threatening letter to Mr David Edie "a farmer at Cornceres" on 15th October, and signing it "JACK THE RIPPER"; another threatening letter on the 22nd signed "CATCH ME IF YOU CAN", and further letters on 22nd October with a further letter written to Mr Russel, the editor of the *East Fife Record*, stating "Catch Me if You Can" and desiring that the letter should be inserted into the weekly paper. Both sets of letters repeated the threats to murder David Edie and his family. The endings and signatures in all the letters mirrored those from the Whitechapel "Jack the Ripper", whose letters written to newspapers had been published and highly publicised throughout the United Kingdom.

The boy was also accused of writing the following letters...

Addressed to the Reverend A. Douglas, the Abbey Minister of Arbroath. Sent from Anstruther 26th Sept 1888.

A further letter bearing the date 1st October posted from Pittenweem. Both letters were signed: "your assassin".

A third letter bearing the date 31st Oct posted in Pittenweem and signed "Rob the Beginner".

A fourth letter dated 16th October – posted from Pittenweem, signed "Your Assassin".

A fifth letter bearing the date 22nd October, signed "Catch Me if You Can". All the letters had been posted and received in due course, as detailed in court, and contained threats to murder the Rev Andrew Douglas.

In the packed courtroom, they heard the accused boy plead, "Not guilty".

> Cross-examined at the Bar by the Procurator Fiscal Mr Renton…
>
> Reverend Douglas testified that on 10th September 1888 his study window was fired into. He had since received a number of threatening letters. Cross-examined, he said:
>
> Answer…Though the outrages had not happened, the letters were of such an insulting and disgusting nature that I would have done all I could to get the author of them!
>
> Question…Then were you terrified and alarmed?
>
> Answer…It depends what you mean.
>
> Question…Were you alarmed by the letters, pure and simple?

Answer...I was alarmed in this sense, that it brought before me some possibility that the outrage in some form might be repeated.

Question...You regarded these letters seriously, notwithstanding their absurdity?

Answer...I did. Evil is very absurd of itself.

Question...Did you think these letters would emanate from a boy, or did you suspect them to come from one?

Answer...I don't think they could have come from a boy without collusion with some other person, for the fact stated of my wife at one time having lived in Grangemuir. No mere boy could have known that fact unless it had been communicated to him.

Question...That reference leads you to think there were more than one party at the bottom of these letters?

Answer...That was my impression, and is my impression still, seeing that I base my opinion very largely on that simple fact.

Question...How long is it since your wife resided at Grangemuir?

Answer...I think it will be twenty-seven or twenty-eight years and she has not been in the habit of visiting there since.

Question...How many threatening letters have you got altogether since the outrage?

Answer...Eleven; five from this district, three

from Arbroath district, two from Dundee, and one from Glasgow.

The prisoner's declaration was read to the court on the 3rd November 1888, in which he denied writing the letters that he had been accused of writing to...Mr Edie, Birrel, Russel, and Rev Douglas. But John Watson did admit writing one letter to Mr Edie, one which did not appear to have reached him.

The Fiscal and the accused's agent having addressed the Sheriff, his lordship said that after evidence which had been read at great length, it was impossible to come to any conclusion, other than that he had written these letters and despatched them for the purpose of annoying the gentlemen.

To put the boy in prison was out of the question. He would only be punishing the parents. In order to impress upon him that it was not to play or trifle with the feelings of others, it was to make him physically suffer. He was at an age where he could not be severely punished, but he was prepared to sentence twelve strokes – with a birch rod!

Although the judge did not think this would be a severe punishment, in fact it would involve being hit on the bare flesh a dozen times with a bundle of switches.

Once this sentence had been delivered, there was another shock for the large crowd in the courtroom. The accused's agent now handed the judge a medical certificate which stated that the state of the accused's health would make it dangerous to visit him with such a physical punishment!

With this the Judge issued a fine of £5, which was immediately paid by the accused's parents.

And so ended the tale of the "JACK THE RIPPER" of Pittenweem. Caught by his handwriting by an intrepid detective from St Andrews police force. Sentenced in the High Sheriff's court of Fife to receive twelve lashes with the birch…promptly reduced to a £5 fine,[*] and released back home to Pittenweem…where I'm sure his own parents delivered a severe punishment also. He was indeed…a very naughty boy! But the Jack the Ripper of Pittenweem's terror was over!

I would be very ignorant about this story without the help from Mr Stewart Evans, who directed me to the two newspapers that highlighted the case…

Dundee Courier, 17 December 1888

Fife Herald, 19 December 1888

---

[*] The average earnings for the late 19th century was 1821 shillings a week (according to William Booth the founder of the Salvation Army) £5 was about a month's wages!

Chapter 28

Kirkoswald's Ministerial Bash

In the parish of Kirkoswald in Ayrshire 1889, a huge opportunity had arisen with the retirement of its last minister.

Way back in 1496 an Act of Parliament from the time of King James III made it compulsory to send the firstborn son of every well-to-do family for schooling. It was done in an effort to combat the high illiteracy in the kingdom. Now for every first-born educated and fresh from university teachings, a suitable job to reflect the teaching was required.

But in Scotland these were few and far between, and only the security of the parish could bring the lucrative benefits that were sought after. So, when an empty seat in an ancient kirk for position of Minister came up, there was always a stampede of applicants for the job!

September 1889 in the parish of Kirkoswald: a village renowned for farming, tile manufacturing, and a small but profitable coal mine. One claim to fame is that Robert Burns went to school there. The village's name had been taken from a Northumbrian warlord who won a battle here in the 7th century. It was an ancient seat of the parish – the church being built in 1244. But in September 1889 another battle was about to be fought!

In September 1889, an important gathering had the church packed with nearly 600 people. It was a church meeting, with deacons set to choose the kirk of Kirkoswald's new parish minister.

But this was the third such meeting, and once again the hours had passed slowly as each applicant was paraded in front of the seniors of the kirk. As with the previous attempts to choose a minister, this third meeting was heading the way of the other two...anticipating the long hours to come, every potential applicant had brought along a wee bit of tonic in a bottle to suppress the nerves. But every applicant had also brought dozens of supporters, who had in turn also brought a bottle with them, and on top of that, most of them had brought a fair amount already...inside them – lots of whisky!

As the hours passed, every new hopeful candidate that came to the deacons' attention was followed by catcalls from the pews of the church, as other suitors bellowed abuse. It soon became a Mexican wave of drunken brawling. An insult too far was answered with violence. Then the two teams of supporters contested the insult full John Wayne style! Before you could say "praise the good Lord!" they had a full-blown riot – clergy hopefuls with their supporters gently and at first with good nature berated the opposition. Then as the mountainous amounts of whisky were consumed, humble apprentice Godly men turned into fully drunken cave men as they contested the job offer with fists and frightful language, in a full-on brawl.

After several hours of trying to suppress the violence, and I'm sure asking God's help several times, the moderator of the meeting had no option but to direct the job application to be cancelled officially for a third time due to the cumulative effect of the rising tensions from these potential professors of religion and their impressive consumption of whisky!

The meeting once again had to be dissolved, with the comment that such disgraceful scenes were common.

The newspapers covered the story all over Scotland. The *Leven Advertiser* covered the story…

> Whenever a pulpit becomes vacant, the congregation splits itself into sections, each of which favours its own candidate and advocates his election with an amount of animosity, rancour and personal abuse which in ordinary communities would entail social ostracism, but in Scotland gains nothing but admiration. Whenever a vacancy occurs, they will move heaven and earth to get their own incubus selected, ignoring the decency, order and the sacred nature of the building in which they meet: the Church.

A month later, on October 3, the *Leven Advertiser* newspaper wrote…

> The Reverend Mr Muir, Largo, was on Monday night unanimously appointed Minister of the parish of Kirkoswald. A repetition of the extraordinary scenes witnessed at the last congregational meeting having been feared, a force of 30 policemen, including a police shorthand writer, were drafted into the village. Fortunately, this time their services

were not needed, proceedings being orderly throughout.

As a Largo man myself, I'm pretty sure Mr Muir could hold his whisky!

Chapter 29

Unterseeboot U-12 Terrorises the North Sea

When the arms race of the early 20th century culminated in the outbreak of hostilities in what would be regarded as "the Great War", the British Empire had little faith in the development of a submarine fleet. Immense amounts of money were going to battleship and dreadnought building instead. Britain ruled the waves, or so the recruitment posters proclaimed, as they promoted a life in the marine forces. But Germany was building warships too and investing heavily in a submarine fleet. They were very expensive to build – the German U-boats cost two million marks.

The First World War submarines were regarded as "iron coffins" and that's from the sailors who sailed in them. There were good reasons for that nickname. The early ones used in this war could only submerge for a total of two hours before the engines (swapped when submerged from diesel to battery-powered electric engines) produced hydrogen gas. After two hours below snorkel depth, the crews would have used up the fresh air; from then on they were being slowly poisoned by invisible fumes. Seventy-two hours of this and the crew on board would all be dead.

And if things sound bad with diesel engines, they were a massive improvement from what was used before! The previous engines aboard a submarine had used paraffin, giving a speed of 14 knots on 1,400 horsepower. But the crews suffered from the fumes and fuel consumption was also extremely high. The diesel engine was seen as a turning point for submarine boat construction.

The submarine could only cruise at sea level until a target was sighted, swap from diesel fuel to battery, and submerge for an attack, hopefully fire its torpedoes, hit its target and get as far away as possible from the victim while underwater, creating a sizeable distance from any chasing destroyers before having to resurface for air.

It didn't help that the batteries were stored beneath the 30-man crew's sleeping quarters. Ventilation failure was common, and the very explosive hydrogen gas accumulating was another explosion risk. In all, 375 *Unterseeboote* were constructed during the First World War by the Germans, and 202 were lost at sea, on active service, through mechanical failure, or in accidents. Of the 17,000 men enlisted into the submarine fleet, 5,100 would never return. In this period 2,600 merchant and Royal Navy vessels would be sunk by the submarine menace.

U-12 was ordered on 15th July 1908 from Kaiserliche Werft Danzig company. It was 57 metres long, 493 tonnes, and carried 6 torpedoes and a crew of 30. It cost 2,140,000 marks to build and had a range of 14,000 kilometres. It had one distinguishing feature, and a surprising one at that: it was built so that a seaplane could sit on deck and when the submarine submerged it would float free and manage to take off under its own power to attack shipping. One major drawback...when the plane's fuel ran low, the pilot could only land back in the sea – a tremendously dangerous situation in North Sea waters. Many pilots must have known they flew to their deaths once free from the submarine.

At the start of the First World War the British had no belief in the future of submarines. They could be easily fired upon from a distance and once submarines were sufficiently damaged it was routine for battleships to put them under for good by ingloriously ramming them. By 1916 the invention of the depth charge provided another method of sinking them. A heavy charge could be dropped overboard to create a major underwater explosion. The concussion was lethal to submarines.

As a first step, on the outbreak of war in 1914, Britain tried to starve Germany of its imports from its African colonies. A naval blockade was enforced, with merchant ships heading to Germany being arrested and taken to British ports. The German reaction was to encircle the British waters and to claim the right to sink all merchant transports destined for UK ports. Neutral countries trading with the UK were warned they would be targeted if found in UK waters. This policy was put into force by February 1915 and the *Unterseeboot* fleets were let loose to police this effect.

George D'Oyly Lyon, who was gunnery officer of HMS *Monarch* during the First World War, later described how British ships would approach a submarine attack, saying that the most effective way of destroying submarines below the surface at that time was by means of a sweep by the ships using hydrophones, and then depth charges. Hydrophones were undersea microphones; any submarine engine noise could be picked up and a reasonable assumption of where the submarine was could be followed up by sea mines or depth charges.

Knowing how little time a submarine could stay under could have a naval response waiting for the first sight of the sub's marine tower.

U-12 first saw action on 11th November 1914 off the coast of Deal, 13 kilometres northeast of Dover, where it successfully targeted and sank the 810-tonne torpedo gunboat *Niger*. U-12 was sighted on the 6th March 1915 about 40 kilometres southeast of Aberdeen by the British trawler *Duster*, a local patrol ship. U-12 managed to dive and escape. The trawler, not being fitted with radio, could only report the incident at dawn when a passing armed yacht *Portia* took the news to Rosyth. With the news, Admiral Sir Robert Lowry, the Commander in Chief of the East Coast forces, set every armed unit of his Peterhead Patrol to join in the hunt for U-12. On the 8th of March she was sighted again!

Off the coast of Cruden Bay, 32 kilometres north of Aberdeen, U-12 had to surface for air. The conditions once submerged can only be imagined, choking on building fumes but knowing that to surface could mean your instant death with hunting frigates above! A minesweeper trawler saw U-12 surface, and she was also caught again heading in a southern direction by a trawler in the evening. She was chased to Stonehaven by the trawler *Martin,* where she submerged again before they could target her with gunfire. Another armed trawler *Chester* took up the chase at 1500 hrs near Montrose where she dived again to get away. Another submarine was reported near Aberdeen, and Sir

Robert Lowry sent out Captain F. Blunt and thirteen destroyers of the 4th Flotilla from Rosyth to sweep northwards towards Aberdeen. When this line of ships made its way out of the Forth Estuary the armoured cruiser HMS *Leviathan* was seen at 1730 to be under attack just 24 kilometres from the Fife coast. She managed to zigzag, and a torpedo missed

Unterseeboot U-12.

her. U-12 had surfaced for the attack but the Rosyth Flotilla had her in range, straddling her with shots before she dived undersea again. The destroyers passed over her with the hydrophone system dragging behind: something was detected so they returned and swept south again. But it seemed she had escaped them. Next morning reports came from a trawler (*May Island*) that a submarine had been sighted again 40 kilometres from Fife Ness.

Three destroyers took up the chase, *Acheron*, *Attack*, and *Ariel*. They formed abreast one mile apart from each other and swept the area with hydrophones. At 1010, the U-12 was sighted as she broke the surface on the horizon two and a half kilometres away.

The ships went full speed as U-12 tried to dive. At 180 metres she was seen, almost submerged, but *Ariel* rammed her. The conning tower took the brunt of the damage, and the U-boat, mortally wounded and letting in water, surfaced to fight it out.

The destroyers with no hesitation opened fire, hitting U-12, and the resulting explosion put the deck gun overboard, killing the crew men on deck. The crew inside panicked to get out, knowing their fate in the stricken sub. A few fought to get on deck holding up hands for surrender. The destroyers ceased hostilities and lowered boats for survivors as the sub started to go down. The submarine quickly sank, taking down 18 crew to their doom, along with their captain, Kapitanleutnant Hans Kratzsch. Only ten men were saved.

The observations of the trawlers had led the destroyers to a successful kill. For their hard work the crews of the *May Island*, *Duster*, *Coote*, *Chester*, and the *Martin* all received rewards, the *May Island* getting £500.

The second submarine sighted off Aberdeen in the chase for U-12 was also sunk on the 18th by a dreadnought. It was evident the U-boats were a foretaste of attacks on the Grand Fleet.

Because of the action of U-boats in sinking merchant ships, the British Admiralty wanted the prisoners from the U-12 treated as pirates. They were put in solitary confinement. Once the German High Seas Command heard this, they responded in kind. Ten British officers were chosen and put in cells 3.5 by 2.5 metres with nothing but a blanket. On the 12th of May the *Times* newspaper described the American ambassador visiting the men in Berlin. (America was not involved in the war at that time.) The ambassador had found the Honourable Alexander A.

Fraser, Master of Saltoun, an officer of the Gordon Highlanders, in a cell – an outrageous treatment of a British officer. Swiss delegates now were called upon to help matters, but he was only released in November 1918. He would become twentieth Lord Saltoun in 1933 and served in the House of Lords till 1963.

In January 2008, deep sea divers Jim McLeod and Martin Sinclair on board the dive ship *North Star* found the wreckage of U-12, 40 kilometres from Eyemouth. It was found 47 metres deep in quite amazing condition. It was a five-year search, and diver Mike Clark was there to photograph the wreck, noting that a nice big lobster had set up home in one of the torpedo tubes. But what was most interesting was two WW1 hydrophones wrapped around the submarine with metal wires. Is this what stopped U-12 from diving when under attack from *Ariel*? Was the submarine already tangled in their hydrophone system?

Further reading

Shipwrecks in the Forth, Bob Baird, p. 114...U-12 details.

Naval Document...1935 Rear Admiral of Third Cruiser Squadron George D'Oyly Lyon...The Sinking of u12

Details on finding the wreck of U-12...Mike Clark... Dive Blog.

Details of British prisoners' treatment after U-12 men captured...Head of Reference service RICS Surveyors institution.

Research...Roger Wilson...Author's special thanks.

Chapter 30

Stranger Danger!
(When Big Sister Knows Best)

A parents first lesson to a child when it ventures outwith the safety of the front door of the house, whether it's with the grandparents or big brothers is…"DON'T TALK TO STRANGERS!"

A simple rule, and in this next story it well could have been a life saver.

In the village of Arncroach near Elie in Fife, September 1965: the village park was in the middle of a football kickabout. The couthy scene had discarded jerseys for goalposts and push bikes lying on their sides as the shouts of a football match was keenly fought by a group of under 10s. Several mums stood by in the busy village, mainly farmer stock and everybody knew each other's business. At the front of the park was a water well where the young lads refreshed themselves after the game.

Today a green minivan was parked nearby, and the owners were filling water bottles from the spring.

The van owners were a couple up from Manchester, the female had yellow bleached hair and seemed to be the chattier of the two. The man seemed oblivious to the children, dark short hair greased back and smart looking in his suit.

One boy 6 years old thought the attractive woman very nice, and she was really friendly she even opened and showed him the inside of the camper van where they slept.

At this point the boy's older sister thought something wasn't quite right and pulled her brother away from the van and the couple, to the woman's annoyance. As big sister ushered him forward towards home, they got a last look at the couple from Manchester as they drove past, taking the route southward out the village.

One month later the couple would-be front-page news in the whole of the UK...known horrifically as the Moor Murderers.

Myra Hindley and Ian Brady were caught and arrested on 7th October 1965, they had been identified as killing 17 year old Edward Evans, bludgeoning him to death with an axe to impress Myra's brother in law...who shopped them to the police! They would eventually be undone by the photos they had been taking on holiday. A curious sergeant wondered why they had bleak meaningless photos on Saddleworth moor with Hindley posing with Cheshire cat grins. Grins that hid a secret. The sergeant found the locations in the photos...and the bodies of murdered children beneath where she stood. Three were found in shallow graves...another child they confessed to killing but has still not yet been found.

The nature of their crimes was abhorrent – all the children were sexually assaulted. A recording was made with the cries of ten year old Lesley Ann Downy crying for her mother as she was tortured; her cries are suddenly stopped as she was hit by Brady...the silence is broken by the music of "the drummer boy" being played in the back ground.

Ian Brady and Myra Hindley in 1965.

St Monans Newark Castle.

One of the Brady photos confused the Police as it showed a coastal doocot in the background with Myra standing posing, another had Brady smiling from an old ruined archway. With the murderers sentenced to life in jail for 5 murders the police never pursued the remaining photos. It wasn't till Ian Brady was declared dead in 2017 that photos came out of the locations.

My last book was THE BATTLE OF ST MONANS...

a big fight on the beach here in 1548 between Scots forces and the English. My photos for the book were taken from the castle location...the location I recognised as the exact spots where both Ian Brady and Myra Hindley had stopped and posed for photos. One month before capture. They had gone south out of Arncroach to nearby St Monans' Newark Castle.

One wee 6 year old boy from Arncroach has a lot to thank his big sister for...if it wasn't for her persistence I may have had another body to talk about, found at Newark Castle

Source...The Arncroach youngster although now in his 50s has asked me to remain anonymous. He is a fan of my books and approached me in 2015 with the story. I had the decency to let him read this before adding to this book to confirm how I wrote it to the truth of the matter...I thank him.

Picture Credits

Front Cover

Urquhart Castle on Loch Ness, © Lian Deng… Dreamstime.com

Chapter 4

Bothwell painting, young man…by Derrick Lunn…Mary Queen of Scots visitor centre

Painting of the corpse of bothwell…OTTO BACHE, 1861, oil on canvas…National Library of Scotland

Chapter 7

Lord Bruce's Heart casket…Lord Stowell…Archaeologia, vol. 20… London, 1824

Chapter 11

Hollyrood fireplace where apprentice cook was eaten…Scot Nat MP Jenny Gilruth

Chapter 15

John Paul engraving…J B Longacre

John Paul Jones corpse…US Naval Institute

John Paul Jones tomb…US Naval Academy

Chapter 19

Sketch of original lighthouse…British Library, Mechanical Curator collection, "Emeralds chased in Gold; or, the Islands of the Forth: their story, ancient and modern." John Dickson, 1899

View of Isle of May…David Stokes, 2006

Chapter 21

Scotland Forever! painting by Elizabeth Thompson, Lady Butler 1881, Leeds Art Gallery

All other images from the author's collection.

CPSIA information can be obtained
at www.ICGtesting.com
Printed in the USA
BVHW071534270321
603572BV00004B/438